Praise for

The Secret Lives of Customers

"Prepare to be hooked! With style, humor, and a lighthearted parable, *The Secret Lives of Customers* will help you see your customers with fresh eyes. Dave Duncan explains the 'jobs to be done' concept better than anyone, and keeps you smiling, nodding, and eagerly turning the pages for more."

—Safi Bahcall, author of the international bestseller *Loonshots*

"A page turner that reads like a mystery but filled with practical insights for sleuthing out what your customers really want. With a cast of characters you'll easily recognize, Duncan's story is a blueprint anyone can use to solve the mysteries of customer behavior."

—Mark Bertolini, former chairman and CEO of Aetna

"A grand slam: an excellent detective story, with key lessons that are easy to grasp and rigorous. Learning to understand customers has never been so much fun—and so easy."

—Jacques Goulet, president of Sun Life Canada

"David Duncan's refreshingly human detective story enlightens and entertains while reminding us that 'small data'—curious conversation, the right questions, and empathy—may be the most powerful tools we have for uncovering what customers want from us."

—Paul LeBlanc, president, Southern New Hampshire University

"The promise of the data and analytics revolution for improving customers' lives can only be realized if it's focused on asking—and answering—the right questions. Duncan provides a blueprint for how to do just this, and does so through an engaging, accessible story that everyone can relate to."

—Brian Cassin, CEO, Experian

"A fresh approach to understanding what customers really want, told through an entertaining detective story. This is essential reading for anyone looking to understand their customers, today and in the future."

—Karen S. Lynch, president and CEO, CVS Health

THE SECRET
LIVES OF
CUSTOMERS

THE SECRET
LIVES OF
CUSTOMERS

A Detective Story
About Solving the
Mystery of Customer Behavior

David Scott Duncan

PublicAffairs
New York

PublicAffairs
Hachette Book Group
1290 Avenue of the Americas, New York, NY 10104
www.publicaffairsbooks.com
@Public_Affairs

Printed in the United States of America

First Edition: May 2021

Published by PublicAffairs, an imprint of Perseus Books, LLC, a subsidiary of Hachette Book Group, Inc. The PublicAffairs name and logo is a trademark of the Hachette Book Group.

The Hachette Speakers Bureau provides a wide range of authors for speaking events. To find out more, go to www.hachettespeakersbureau.com or call (866) 376-6591.

The publisher is not responsible for websites (or their content) that are not owned by the publisher.

Library of Congress Cataloging-in-Publication Data
Names: Duncan, David Scott (Business consultant), author.
Title: The secret lives of customers : a detective story about solving the mystery
    of customer behavior / David Scott Duncan.
Description: First edition. | New York : PublicAffairs, [2021]
Identifiers: LCCN 2020049992 | ISBN 9781541774490 (hardcover) |
    ISBN 9781541774483 (ebook)
Subjects: LCSH: Marketing research—Case studies. | Consumer behavior—
    Case studies. | Customer relations—Case studies.
Classification: LCC HF5415.2 .D86 2021 | DDC 658.8/342—dc23
LC record available at https://lccn.loc.gov/2020049992

ISBNs: 978-1-5417-7449-0 (hardcover); 978-1-5417-7448-3 (ebook)

LSC-C

Printing 1, 2021

For Suzanne and Zoe

Contents

PROLOGUE

I f you want to understand customers, start by thinking like a detective.

I've long believed the art of understanding what customers want and why they do what they do has much in common with how a detective goes about solving a mystery. Customers are endlessly surprising, often acting in ways that don't seem to make sense and presenting, for a time at least, a mystery to be solved. A market mystery, if you will. When this happens, the best response is to look around for clues about what's going on—by talking to people, observing them, gathering data, identifying patterns, and drawing out insights that suggest the right next step.

Just like a detective.

Solid market detective skills are more needed than ever, and not just by people in specialized research departments. The maxim "The customer is boss" has become only more urgent as the digital revolution, social media, expanding

1

choices, and 24/7 connectivity have empowered consumers and heightened their expectations for any experience with a product, company, or brand. This means nearly *everyone*— including those working in executive leadership, marketing, product development, sales, customer service, and even departments such as HR or finance—needs to be constantly attuned to what customers want today and in the future.

What's surprising, then, is the absence of an effective approach to cracking market mysteries that anyone can learn and apply in a wide variety of situations. To be sure, powerful methods exist within the confines of market research (or, increasingly, data science) departments. But they are too specialized to be useful to most people working in the business world. More fundamentally, the result is often a deluge of data and analysis that, however sophisticated it may appear, falls short of the insights needed to truly improve customers' lives.

My goal with *The Secret Lives of Customers* is to fill this gap by teaching a language, method, and mindset that equips *anyone* to understand the customers they serve (or want to serve). At its heart is the simple but profound idea that what drives customer behavior is the existence of important, unsatisfied "jobs" they are looking to get done. When these jobs arise, people look around for the best products, services, or experiences to "hire" to solve for them. Therefore, the top priority of any aspiring market detective should be learning how to discover, understand, and solve for these jobs.

This book shows you how through two very different parts:

- Part I, "The Case of the Disappearing Customers," is a story about a leadership team confronted with a "market mystery" that threatens the future of their organization. Although fictional, it's highly representative of real-world challenges faced by most organizations today. The skills and tools of the market detective are illustrated as the plot unfolds, and you see how solving a market mystery actually develops from beginning to end.
- Part II, "Becoming a Market Detective," steps out of the story and explains in more detail the concepts, techniques, and tools used to "crack the case," including how they can be applied to a wide range of real-world situations.

My hope is that you will find this book both useful and enjoyable, whether you work through it individually or with a team. And I hope it helps you to solve your own market mysteries, whatever they may be.

David Scott Duncan

PART I

The Case of the Disappearing Customers

The day the Mayor disappeared was the day Cate Forrest knew she had a big problem.

Ed Amato had been a regular at the Tazza Cafe ever since Cate launched it twelve years earlier. Every Saturday morning and most weekdays he'd amble into Tazza's main Boston location just as it opened, greet the familiar baristas, and perch on the same high seat at the long coffee bar. Though he invariably carried the daily paper, not once in twelve years had anyone seen him open it. He preferred to spend his time talking—with the staff, other regulars, people just passing through—anyone within earshot. His zest for conversation and genuine curiosity about people made him instantly likable, and his habit of making everyone feel welcome earned him the affectionate nickname "the Mayor."

As Cate's company grew, Ed was there at all the important milestones. At the one-year anniversary he was the first to toast the team, raising his favorite coffee mug in Tazza's honor. When Cate opened her second location, Ed came for the ribbon cutting, joking that he'd need to spend some time there to break the place in. He was there at each subsequent opening, including the most recent, the fourteenth. And Cate had expected Ed would be part of the celebration after Tazza completed an initial public offering—an IPO—in two months' time and raised the funding to go national.

But then, one Saturday morning in early April, Ed disappeared.

At first everyone assumed he was out of town. Even Ed, they reasoned, must have a life outside Tazza. But when he didn't appear the next day, or the following week, the close-knit cafe community became concerned. Regulars grilled the head barista, James Finley. Was Ed sick? Did he have an accident? But James was as surprised as anyone and had no answers. Ed's disappearance was so noteworthy that James brought it up in his weekly planning meeting with Cate.

"Ed's gone," James announced as he walked into her office.

Cate looked up from a stack of legal documents with a worried expression.

"Is he OK?"

"I guess so. He hasn't been in for two weeks. Everyone's been asking about him, but no one knew anything . . . until yesterday." James hesitated, reluctant to share the news. "Harriet saw him rushing out of the Second Street Stella's after lunch. When she called his name, he crossed the street and rushed away. Harriet thinks he was avoiding her. She swears he looked guilty."

"Stella's! He should feel guilty. Going to that generic chain."

Cate took a moment to process this news, then sighed. "Terrible timing. Have you seen where our quarterly numbers are heading?"

James nodded with a frown. As head barista, he was close enough to daily operations to sense where sales were trending, and it was in the wrong direction.

With only two months before the IPO, Cate knew every market signal would be scrutinized—especially by Tazza's bankers. They were eager to pitch Tazza as a growth story with nearly unlimited potential given its fanatical fan base and small regional presence. But as much as bankers are prone to positive spin, Cate knew any bad news would impact the valuation and could even threaten the IPO.

Lost in thought, Cate let her gaze drift around the room and alight on the two most inspirational pictures in her office. The first was of her two toddlers, Sophie and Jack, working with endearing concentration to create a sculpture on the beach near their New England home while her husband watched over and beamed with pride. The second was of Cate standing next to her best friend, Emma, in front of a small cafe in Florence, Italy, holding the napkin on which they'd sketched out the original idea for Tazza.

Making a decision, she picked up a package of marketing material she'd been studying earlier that morning, looking for the contact number. "Alex Baker & Co., Market Detectives," it read at the top, with the tagline "Don't let your customers remain a mystery." *Unusual branding*, Cate thought, but the firm had been recommended by her board chairman and old family friend, Ethan Raynor, and she trusted his judgment. And she knew she was running out of time.

"Well, as I always say, 'If you want to do something different, you have to *do* something different.'"

She picked up the phone and called the number.

1

ONBOARDING

B aristas are the bartenders of the twenty-first century."
Alex Baker pondered the truth of these words, written in green chalk at the top of an expansive menu board
listing the daily Tazza Cafe specials, as he waited for Cate
Forrest to arrive. After a series of phone conversations, Alex
had agreed to work with Cate on what he called a "market
investigation" into Tazza's situation. If he had any doubts
about signing up, they vanished when he listened to a voice-
mail from Tazza board member and mutual friend Ethan
Raynor.

"Alex. Ethan. I have someone who could use your help.
Old friend and best leader I've ever met. And it's for one of
your favorite causes: coffee."

Now Alex sat at the main bar at Tazza's flagship location,
a converted loft space overlooking the harbor on the edge
of Boston's North End. He had read a bit on the history of
Tazza, its roots in this historic Boston neighborhood, and its

rapid expansion into the suburbs of nearby northeastern cities. He had read about Cate as well, and was looking forward
to meeting her, as she was widely regarded as an excellent
leader and resourceful entrepreneur.

It was Cate who had suggested this location, her favorite spot for business meetings. The open vista of the ocean
spotted with drifting white sails always helped Cate to put
problems into their proper perspective. Alex was absorbed in
this view as Cate approached.

"Hello, Alex! Apologies for being late. Boston traffic."

As Alex stood to shake her hand, Cate was surprised by
his appearance. Perhaps she had expected a self-described
"market detective" to have the no-nonsense demeanor of
the crime fighters populating the stories her father, a life-
long mystery fan, had read to her when she was young. But
if anything, Alex seemed more like one of her old college
professors, with his observant expression and soft-spoken
confidence. Not surprising, she supposed, for someone with
a master's degree in psychology who had left a graduate program for the business world nearly two decades earlier. She'd
done her homework on Alex as well.

"I'm pleased you'll be working with us, Alex. You come
highly recommended. I thought we could use this meeting
to get to know each other better. I'd love to learn more about
how you work, and I can fill in some background. But first
things first: Can I get you a coffee?"

Alex needed little prompting to indulge in his favorite
drink. "Yes, thanks. I'll have—"

"Excuse me! Sebastian—can we get two coffees please!" Cate shouted.

Alex looked accustomed to more elaborate orders, so Cate explained. "When it comes to coffee, I'm used to doing things the Italian way. You order a coffee in Italy, you get only one thing—an espresso made from the house beans. Robusta—or Arabica if you're lucky. Ideally you drink it at a coffee bar like this one, so we've got that covered. It's a ritual that might recur multiple times a day—kind of marks the rhythms of daily life over there."

"Interesting," Alex murmured to himself with a thoughtful expression. He even opened his notebook and jotted something down, a gesture not lost on Cate.

"I see you are already making observations, Alex. Tell me—how did you end up as a 'market detective'?"

Alex closed his notebook and carefully set it aside before replying. "In a rather roundabout way, I suppose. I've always been fascinated by people. Even as a kid I loved listening to them tell their stories—or reading about them. Ended up in college studying psychology and anthropology, then started a graduate program combining the two. But after a couple of years, university life started to feel too removed from reality. I longed to do something more applied. So at the old age of thirty I dropped out."

At that moment the barista, a young woman wearing ripped jeans, a black Tazza T-shirt, and a name tag reading "Jessie," approached with their order. Without a word she deposited two cups of espresso in front of them and floated away to her next task. Cate frowned at the lack of interaction but said nothing. Alex continued.

"Then I got lucky. A kindly professor introduced me to the manager of a market research group at a big media company. They were developing new ways to learn about their customers, and it turned out my education was surprisingly relevant. I spent eight happy years there, learning about all the latest research methods and helping to develop some new ones."

Alex paused to take a sip of his coffee, exhaling audibly as he savored the flavor. "I might have stayed longer, but life got in the way. In a good way, I should add. I got married, we had twins, moved across the country to be close to family. I decided to take a chance and start my own consulting business. That's when I came up with the idea of billing myself as a 'market detective.'

"I've always thought the work of understanding customers is similar to the work detectives do. Our clients come to us because there is something happening in the world they don't understand—what I call *market mysteries*. Our job is to go into these markets, make observations, interview people—to gather clues as to what's going on. Then we look for patterns, insights, and ultimately piece together information to solve the mystery. Just like detectives trying to crack a case."

"Makes sense," Cate said. "I love the branding. Also adds a bit of drama to the work, eh?"

"Indeed," Alex agreed. "Of course our work doesn't typically involve crimes, villains, or victims, but the work of searching for clues, interpreting them, and piecing together a puzzle is very similar. For example, I see that you've had a lot of unexpected turnover in your barista staff recently."

"How did you know that?" asked Cate, surprised. They were, in fact, dealing with a wave of recent departures.

"Observation—and a bit of guesswork. The young woman who delivered our coffee—she barely acknowledged you when she delivered our drinks. You, the founder and CEO of the company! No employee who had been around for long with any sense of career preservation would act that way. She must not know who you are, and therefore must be new. You shouted 'Sebastian' with our coffee order; it's reasonable to assume this young woman was not who you expected. Finally, since this is your largest, busiest location, I assume you'd want to have the most experienced baristas working here. Having someone so new suggests there are problems at other locations as well."

Cate was impressed. "It seems obvious when you explain it," she said.

"Well, a famous researcher once said, 'The world is full of obvious things which nobody by any chance ever observes.'"

"Business school was a long time ago, Alex. Was that one of your marketing professors?"

"No. Sherlock Holmes. *The Hound of the Baskervilles.* You'll find that he has much to say on the art of the market detective."

"Ha! I like this way of thinking about it," said Cate. "So what are the most common market mysteries you are hired to solve?"

Alex took another sip while reflecting on his answer. "Every mystery is different, but they all tend to start the same way: Leaders notice something happening in their market that is highly unexpected. Something that can't be explained by the usual lens through which they view the world. Maybe it's longtime, loyal customers disappearing or defecting to a competitor. Maybe a new type of competitor arrives on the scene and starts to grow rapidly. Or maybe it's a positive change that still seems impossible to understand, like new types of customers buying their products or using them in ways they've never seen."

Alex sensed Cate could relate to these examples, as she was listening intently.

"At first these events might be small, infrequent—easy to ignore. But as they become more common a kind of tension builds—between how those leaders understand the world, and what is actually happening around them. It's like they are used to playing one game, with rules they understand—including how to win it—and then the game itself changes, without any notice as to what the new rules are."

Cate was struck by how familiar this sounded. "That's *exactly* how it feels from my point of view with Tazza. Honestly, until about six months ago everything seemed almost too straightforward. I don't mean it was easy—our success came from many people working very hard over many years. But our basic strategy always stayed the same. In your words, we understood the game we were playing and how to win it. And we were just on this great growth path. Until recently."

She gestured toward a cluster of sailboats on the horizon. "It's like the winds of the market have shifted, but we keep trying to sail in the same old direction. And we don't understand what's happening—or why."

For a moment Cate remembered all that was at stake over the next few months. Not just for her, but for the employees who had invested so much to get the company to this moment. The IPO would provide Tazza with the resources to continue to grow, provide stable and rewarding jobs for the people Cate cared so much about, and expand to touch many more lives with the company mission she believed deeply in. Now all that was at risk.

But Cate was not one to dwell on the negative and snapped back to the urgency of their project. "So how do you go about cracking these mysteries? I hired a new head of marketing, Rob Butler, from one of the big beverage companies about six months ago, and he's been analyzing a ton of new data on our customers and sales. Should I connect you with him?"

Alex grimaced slightly at this suggestion but responded diplomatically. "Data can be immensely powerful—but only if you are looking at the world through the right lens. With the wrong lens, data will just create more confusion. Or worse, it will reinforce a flawed view of reality."

"That's twice you've mentioned this idea of a different lens. What do you mean by that?"

Alex responded by picking up his espresso cup and gesturing toward Cate's. "Let me give you an example. Consider these two delicious cups of coffee we've been drinking.

Moments ago we—or rather, you—made a decision to purchase them. Why?"

Cate felt like she was back in business school being cold called, but since her memories of her MBA years were happy ones, she didn't mind playing along.

"Well, if you ask Rob, he'd say it's because we have the best coffee in the area. He'd say the variety is important too, so we can appeal to anyone—that's why he's greatly expanded our drink menu. Now we have a wide variety of not just coffee drinks, but teas, juices, even alcoholic beverages in some places. He also expanded our food menu so you can pair your drink with whatever you feel like eating."

"OK. So that's Rob's view. What's yours?"

Cate thought for a moment. "I suppose in my case it's because I just love coffee. I love the smell, the taste, the experience. And it's associated with all kinds of happy memories—of traveling, being with friends, of memorable and important business meetings. Doesn't hurt that it gives me a kick of energy and makes me feel more alert. It's also a kind of social custom. We are here together, and I feel like I'm hosting you, so buying you a cup of coffee is part of the meeting ritual. Is that a good answer, Professor?"

"Please—call me Alex. And of course you know far more about your business than I do. I will say that I like your answer much better than Rob's. His answer implies he thinks it's the *products* you sell that cause people to purchase them. 'We have great coffee, therefore people buy it.' I call this the *product-centric* lens for viewing the world.

"But products can't *cause* you to do anything. They are just a means to an end. There are always deeper forces at work that drive behavior. Problems we need to solve, or goals we want to accomplish. I think about these as 'jobs' we are trying to get done. And when these jobs arise we look around for the best products or solutions to 'hire' to get them done—just like we might hire a person to do a job like fixing a leaky pipe in our home or babysitting our kids."

Alex downed the rest of his espresso, then placed the empty cup on the table between them. "So if you want to understand why customers do what they do—for example, why they hire a cup of your excellent coffee—you first have to understand the jobs they are trying to get done. You have to view them through a *jobs-centric* lens and not a product-centric one. It might seem like a small shift in perspective, but in fact it's a profound one—because it focuses your investigations on what's really driving customer behavior and the decisions they make: the important, unsatisfied jobs in their lives."

Cate was intrigued. "So in my case, the jobs I hire coffee for might be 'getting an energy boost,' 'reconnecting with happy memories,' and 'engaging in a kind of ritual for a business meeting.'"

"Precisely. That's why I like your answer—you spoke in terms of the jobs you are trying to get done. Some are more functional, like 'get an energy boost'; others are emotional, like 'connecting with a memory.' And some might be social, as in your business ritual example."

Cate built on the idea further. "I suppose if we can hire products, we can also fire ones that no longer get the job done."

"Yes! Customer jobs are at the heart of any business success—or failure. If more people hire your products to solve their jobs, your business grows; if they fire them, your business shrinks."

Cate felt energized by the idea of looking at Tazza's situation through this new lens. "I assume that must be the focus of your market investigation, then—to understand why customers hire us and why they fire us."

"That's right. All market investigations start by answering those questions. Once we do, we should have a clear picture of what's really going on with Tazza today—which is what you and your team need to figure out how to respond."

"How do you go about answering those questions?" Cate asked.

"We'll use a number of well-tested methods. The best one is also the simplest: talking to people. Current customers, or former ones. Though as with most things, to understand the present it's often instructive to look at the past. Specifically— why did people hire Tazza back when it first started?"

"OK. Where do you start? Who do you need to go interview or investigate first?"

Alex smiled. "The answer is quite convenient, since we are sitting here together: you."

2

ORIGIN STORY

Two rounds of coffee later (which Cate now ordered with the self-conscious thought *Why am I doing this?*), the story of Tazza's origin was coming into focus. Along the way Alex had the opportunity to witness Cate reset the attitude of Jessie, the wayward barista, and coach her to a newfound appreciation for the art of customer service. That Cate could do this in a way that left Jessie inspired and not the least bit defensive made Alex admire her leadership skills all the more.

To orient the conversation, Alex asked Cate to think back on the period of time before she'd first had the idea for Tazza and describe the details of where she was, what she was doing, and what her mindset was—as if she were setting the scene for a movie that was about to begin.

He explained: "Often the people who best understand the jobs a company gets hired for are those who were around at the beginning. These people—founders, entrepreneurs, early employees—must have created a good solution for *some* set of customer jobs or their business wouldn't have taken off. Often their inspiration came from jobs *they* were trying to get done in their own lives. It's a useful starting point to look for clues."

Cate chose to begin her story with the start of her trip to study abroad in Florence, Italy. She had just turned twenty-one and had completed her first two years studying economics and finance at a small New England college, far from the rural town in Michigan where she grew up. She'd never been out of the country, but was inspired by a flyer for a study-abroad program with images of the Tuscan countryside, Florentine art masterpieces, and groups of photogenic students conversing intently with wineglasses and books close at hand. She decided on the spot to go abroad. This intrigued Alex.

"That seems like a big move," he observed. "Heading to Europe for a whole year and leaving behind your friends, the familiar campus. Into the complete unknown. Why did you decide to do that?"

Cate reflected for a moment, then answered. "I think it was precisely that unknown aspect of going to Italy that attracted me. Like I needed a change, perhaps a big change, and this fit the bill. I was pretty focused on my studies for the first two years. I was almost done with the courses for my economics major, with lots of electives to fill in. I figured why not spend a year studying things like art, history, and literature in one of the most beautiful cities in the world?"

Alex nodded but followed up. "Why do you think you needed a change?"

This time Cate had to think longer before answering. "Most people look back on their college days with nostalgia, but my first two years were not too memorable. It's not that they were bad or unhappy, I just spent most of my time studying and kind of floating through the experience. I had friends, even a boyfriend for a while, and they all seemed to be having the time of their lives. Sucking the marrow out of every moment—was it Thoreau who said that? Or at least the beer out of every keg. But I felt removed from all that, so leaving maybe wasn't as hard for me as it might have been for others."

"Why do you think that was?"

Again with the "why" questions! Cate couldn't help noting this. "Before I answer I have a why question for you—why do you keep asking me why?"

Alex explained, "If you're trying to understand the real jobs someone is trying to get done, you often have to get beneath the surface of the first answers you receive. The easiest way to do that is to keep asking why until you get to the fundamental jobs. Some people say you should ask 'five levels of why' to get to it—but it usually doesn't take that many."

Cate imagined this must be what talking to a therapist felt like, but she was committed to the process, so she continued.

"You know, my life now is quite blessed. I have a great family, friends, and work that I love and believe in. But back then I suppose I was still searching for my place in the world. I guess that's normal for most people that age, but it felt more urgent for me somehow. My mother passed away when I was really young, and my father and I moved around a lot for his job while I was growing up. We never did quite lay down roots, so perhaps I was still looking for a sense of community somewhere. I didn't feel it where I was, so maybe I thought I might find it in Italy."

"Ah!" Alex exclaimed. "Now we are getting somewhere. I find that highly significant. But let's continue. What happened once you got to Florence?"

Cate recalled how overwhelmed by new sensations she'd felt upon arriving in Florence. Of course, there were the famous landmarks—the statue of David, Botticelli's Venus ("'Venus on a half shell,' we called it"), the Ponte Vecchio, the Santa Croce church. But most striking was the living artwork that was the city itself, teeming with people and languages from all over the world, every building and avenue hinting at its own ancient story. She loved to wander the city for hours with no destination in mind, just absorbing the voices and sounds and scenes of daily life, and then at night passing by and peering into the brightly lit restaurant and cafe windows swarming with *la dolce vita*.

"I still felt like I was searching for something, but there was this wonderful sense of possibility. All that freedom, beauty—it was exciting. Have you ever been there?"

Alex shook his head. "Did Thoreau also say, 'Traveling is a fool's paradise?' I don't actually believe that, I love to travel. Just never got around to Florence."

"It was Emerson," Cate corrected him. "But close enough. I don't believe it either—especially when it comes to Florence. It was like the city was this great current of life that could carry you along if only you could find a way to jump into its flow. I didn't discover how right away, but that all changed the day I met Emma Gracey."

"The cofounder of Tazza."

"Yes."

"Tell me how that happened."

"Every day when I walked home from class I would pass by a place called Marco's. It was a typical Italian cafe, with a small patio of tables, chairs, and umbrellas for the sun with famous Italian brand names on them. Sometimes I'd stop there and get a drink, but wouldn't linger. Always the same group of people there, or nearly so, and they always seemed to be in these animated conversations—often about soccer—or 'football,' as they call it. They showed the games on a TV you could see from the patio. But my Italian was pretty bad so it didn't feel very welcoming.

"One day in the fall, when it was still warm out, I walked by and there was a woman sitting at one of the tables outside wearing a UMass T-shirt and reading a book in English. It was pretty obvious she was American and she looked about my age, so I introduced myself. That was Emma. It turned out she was studying abroad too, and seemed to be at a similar crossroads. We started talking and have never really stopped talking since. About books, people, life, everything. Now it's about our kids and careers, how hard it is to balance everything. But we are still talking."

Alex had been listening intently and taking notes throughout Cate's story. When she paused he looked up and asked, "So why was meeting Emma so significant?"

This time Cate recognized the "levels of why" technique. "Everything changed after that. Emma helped me find a community there—at, of all places, Marco's. She's more ex- troverted than I am, and her Italian was a lot better, so she knew everyone already. Including the owner, Marco. He was this old Italian guy with the energy of a twenty-year-old— even though he had six grandkids. She introduced me to all the regulars. I'd thought they were standoffish, but once I got to know them they became like a big family. We'd see the same faces every day, and follow the little and big things that happened in their lives. And they'd follow ours. After a while it started to feel like a home."

"Sounds wonderful," said Alex. "How did you have the idea to start a cafe together?"

"One day toward the end of my trip Emma and I were sitting around at Marco's and feeling a bit down about having to leave soon. What had started as a leap into the unknown had turned into this transformative, wonderful ex- perience, and suddenly neither of us wanted to leave. It was Emma who first had the idea, and she put it like this: What if instead of leaving the cafe life behind, we take it with us to the US?

"We were immediately convinced it was a brilliant idea. Of course we were blessed with the naive enthusiasm of people who had never started a business before—but as I tell budding entrepreneurs, this is one of the greatest gifts an entrepreneur can have! Since we were both going back to the Boston area for school, we decided to start it here. We got really lucky. Emma 'knew a guy who knew a guy,' and before long we had funding to open a first place in a converted loft office space in the North End. It became so popular, we were able to expand into this bigger space we are in now."

"Why do you think it became so popular?" Alex asked.

Cate reflected for a moment. "I guess it was like a repeat of my experience in Florence, only this time I was on the other side. Boston attracts people from all over the country, and the world, really. Lots of students here. The first Tazza became a kind of meeting place for all these expats. I think they liked seeing the same faces every day, and that they could plug into a local neighborhood with a long and stable history. Gave them a sense of place. It was a ton of work, but I wouldn't change a thing."

Cate's pride in what she'd built over the years was palpable, and Alex didn't blame her. "Building something from nothing is never easy—no matter what the initial obstacles are. I have enormous respect for anyone who can do it."

"Thank you," Cate said with a smile. "So, Mr. Market Detective: Are these the clues you are looking for?"

Alex looked up from his notes. "It's a great start. It sounds to me like what drew you to that small cafe in Florence was a search for community, and perhaps a place to call home. That's similar to what attracted people to Tazza in the beginning. Using our jobs language, we could say they hired Tazza for the job of 'be part of a community.' This job was particularly important for people in the circumstance of being expats in some sense. People away from home for extended periods of time, for school or work, for example. And you've suggested some aspects of the Tazza experience that made it a great solution for their jobs, for example a consistent group of people to engage with over time."

"That sounds right," Cate agreed. "I'd add one other feature that was important: There had to be a connection to the local culture somehow. Meaning, it couldn't be *all* expats, or some generic place. At Marco's there were lots of locals mixed in, and the environment obviously had all kinds of authentically Italian touches. Those things made you feel connected to the city—and the history—outside the cafe. So over time you started to feel grounded there—like you were more of a citizen and not just a visitor. Our cafes create that same feeling—plenty of longtime residents in the crowd, and each café has a custom look and feel that reflects the surrounding neighborhood."

"Excellent," said Alex. "Very insightful. One other question—why the name Tazza?"

Cate spoke warmly of what was clearly a fond memory. "*Tazza* means 'cup' in Italian. It was inspired by my apartment in Florence, a tiny one-bedroom on the top floor of an old home that had been turned into student lodging. It was really just a converted attic. It was so small, but cozy, and had these old stone walls painted with this lovely, soft Mediterranean-orange color. Across the ceiling you could see traces of little drawings previous students had made that had been painted over. One inspired our name—and was destined to become our logo."

Cate gestured toward an image on the wall of two cups intersecting in a kind of coffee-mug Venn diagram. "That's the same picture that was on my ceiling. There was a little

Italian saying beneath it, *non potemo avere perfetta vita senza amici.* It means 'We cannot have a perfect life without friends.' It's from Dante. You know he was a native of Florence before he was exiled? Probably the most famous native. It all seemed like a sign—Dante speaking to us from the past."

Alex appreciated how thoughtful Cate was about Tazza's purpose and how all the pieces fit together. But Cate was eager to understand where this was all heading.

"So what next? I assume you want to talk to the marketing team to understand what they've learned to date?"

Alex looked mildly shocked at this suggestion, then seemed to choose his words carefully. "Well . . . I'd prefer to go into the field first and form my own conclusions. It's important to be unbiased in these investigations, so I typically avoid talking to company insiders at this stage."

Cate seemed to acquiesce but was a few steps ahead of Alex. "I understand. But I would like you to take along someone who is not a longtime insider and who I think will be helpful. Her name is Jordan Sims. She joined us about six months ago as a market research analyst. She's only twenty-three—graduated from the University of Michigan computer science department."

Alex looked doubtful. He was not used to having a sidekick, certainly not one so inexperienced.

Cate sensed Alex's skepticism. "I think you'll find she's in no way biased or carrying preconceptions," she said. "Also, she's the smartest person in the company."

3

BIG DATA

The next morning Alex went in search of the Smartest Person in the Company. Tazza's suburban headquarters was in a large warehouse converted into trendy new office spaces with high ceilings, exposed ductwork, and sparse furnishings. Alex knew the wide-open floor plans were intended to encourage collaboration and convey a lack of corporate hierarchy, but he wondered how anyone could get any work done with so few barriers to interruption.

After getting directions from what seemed an overly lax security desk, he wound through a labyrinth of cubicles until he found the marketing department. His first clue that he'd succeeded in his quest was seeing a nameplate reading "Jordan Sims" on a cubicle. *Brilliant detective work*, he thought.

There was no door, so he knocked on the wall just behind her, but got no response. With headphones implanted and an audible bass pounding into her ears, Jordan was absorbed in a large screen full of symbols and data that shifted upward every few seconds as her fingers flicked rapidly across the keyboard. Unlike those around her, she was not sitting, her laptop elevated on a standing desk. Her hands paused only every few moments to pick up her Tazza coffee mug and take a sip in what appeared to be a kind of automated behavioral subroutine.

Cate had described Jordan as an expert in the latest big data techniques, and she had a serious, studious look behind her thick glasses that suggested her young lifetime had been spent not just staring at complex symbols on screens, but manipulating and mastering them.

Alex moved into her peripheral vision and waved to get her attention. "Excuse me, are you Jordan Sims?" he asked.

Jordan removed her headphones and turned to assess Alex with the same look he imagined she had when trying to make sense of a newly generated chart of unfamiliar data.

"Yup," she replied. "What's up?"

"I'm Alex Baker. Cate Forrest hired me to investigate why Tazza has been losing customers. I'm heading out to do some interviews. With people I mean," he felt compelled to add for some reason. "Cate suggested you could come along and help out."

Jordan displayed no emotion as she processed this new information. To Alex's surprise, she didn't appear to question his presence, his mission, or her newly discovered role in it.

"Cool. Want to see something interesting?"

Without waiting for a response, she launched a virtuosic salvo of keystrokes and pulled up a series of charts on her monitor.

"I've been trying to understand why Tazza's losing customers too. Rob—he's my boss—asked me to analyze our customer data for the past twelve years to look for useful patterns. What coffee drinks they like best, what they don't like, when they buy it, their demographics—that sort of thing. We have a huge number of products. Guess how many different drinks we sell when you permute all the variables like bean type, drink style, milk versus cream versus soy, or flavoring or whatever?" She didn't wait for Alex to respond. "Twelve thousand five hundred thirty-four. That's nothing compared to Stella's: they have more than eighty thousand different drinks."

Jordan continued to type rapidly and flip charts around on the screen while she spoke. "That's too many drinks to make sense of, so I wrote a sorting algorithm to put them in different buckets we can analyze. Classic coffee drinks, fancy coffee drinks, teas—a few others. Pretty basic, really. Tazza has some good data but it's in a kind of sloppy old-school data lake. I'm recommending we replace it with a master data management architecture I'm designing on the weekends."

"I see," said Alex, not seeing at all.

Another flick of the fingers, and a window popped out with a slide presentation on it titled "Coffee Connoisseurs' Club."

"Now here's the interesting part. Rob launched this program called the Coffee Connoisseurs' Club—I call it the CCC—about six months ago, just after he arrived. The idea was to identify our best customers and find ways to reward them. Had something similar at his last gig and he said it was a big success.

"I helped him set it up. Designed a search algorithm to find these customers. Looks at things like purchase frequency, average level of spend, how long they've been around, do they recommend us to others. Essentially they are the people who spend the most and hang around the cafes the most. Once you're in the CCC you get discounts, accumulate points, free stuff, invites to special events—standard loyalty program stuff. Pretty basic, really."

Alex was beginning to sense that many things were "pretty basic" to Jordan.

"The CCC was a really big initiative," she continued. "It didn't turn sales around, but Rob thinks it has slowed the decline. He's pretty sure the problem is the quality and variety of our coffee drinks, like we can't compete with the big chains given all the choices they have. So I've been analyzing what type of coffee the Connoisseurs like the most. Most favorite, least favorite drinks, does it change depending on the season or time of day? We just launched a survey to ask them how we can create more appealing coffee drinks."

Alex continued to gaze studiously at Jordan's screen. Numbers had never been his strong suit, and he felt his longtime mental allergy to them begin to manifest itself as a kind of uncomfortable itch in his brain.

"Here's what I found out about the CCC members," Jordan said as she twisted her monitor to make it easier for Alex to see. "I just saw it this morning, so I haven't shown it to anyone yet."

Alex moved to get a closer look at the screen, where Jordan had minimized all the other windows and pulled up a single chart. It showed the spending preferences of the Connoisseurs, organized by the categories of products Jordan had defined.

Even Alex could immediately see why Jordan found this chart so interesting.

"But this shows—"

"Yup," Jordan said before Alex could finish. "Seventy-eight percent of the people in our Coffee Connoisseurs' Club—the people who spend the most at Tazza—have never bought a single cup of coffee."

After letting this sink in for a few moments, Alex said, "I think Rob's club might be mislabeled."

"Yup," Jordan said as she took another sip of her drink.

4

STAFF MEETING

Rob Butler sat alone in the Tazza boardroom waiting for his colleagues on the leadership team to arrive for their weekly check-in. The room was smaller—and shabbier—than he was used to, but he expected they'd upgrade after the IPO.

Everyone late as usual, Rob thought. *Massimo will try to run things since he thinks he's second in command.* Cate was traveling for meetings with suppliers, so the rest of the team was on its own today.

Massimo Portinari was head of sales and had the distinction of being employee number one at the company. He was widely liked and respected by the Tazza workforce, though Rob viewed this as due to tenure and not merit. Massimo also had the habit of sprinkling Italian folk wisdom into every conversation, a trait most people found endearing but Rob found irritating.

In fact, Rob's respect for his colleagues went only so far. He viewed himself as the only one with leadership experience in a "real company," having ascended the corporate marketing ladder up to the third-highest rung at a major global sports-drink firm. He did appreciate the work that had been done to build Tazza from nothing, but was shocked when he arrived by how far behind they were in implementing modern, data-driven marketing techniques. For Rob, it made Tazza's initial success hard to understand.

He was less surprised that success had stalled in recent months, and firmly believed he was the one who could turn things around. Most of the projects underway to drive growth were Rob's ideas, and he was eager to take credit for these in the eyes of Cate and the board. At times he even entertained the idea that he might inherit the CEO role after the IPO, once these initiatives proved successful and everyone realized the higher stakes of their new scale.

If they're going to move into the big leagues, they need someone running things with big-league experience.

Rob's thoughts were interrupted by the arrival of the rest of the team, talking animatedly like the old friends they were. Massimo walked in first, followed by Elena Alvarez, CFO, and Kelly Livaria, head of product development. Close behind was Marcus Blaine, head of HR, and lastly James Finley, the head barista, who had recently taken on the role of partnership development. The size of the team, only seven people, was still quite small by big-company standards.

As usual, Massimo was in midspeech. "This game of baseball. I do not understand how you Americans can sit for hours watching these men in the tight pants and the little hats fight over that tiny white ball. Who can even see it? Then once in a while they run around in a circle." Massimo had been to a baseball game the night before for a sales event and was still recovering. "Have you seen a football match? It is art and *scienza* and sport all in one. *Il bel gioco.* The beautiful game."

Elena and James, both diehard baseball fans, rolled their eyes. Massimo lowered his voice and took a serious tone. "You must know there was a little boy standing in the row in front of me. He dropped one of those . . . *hot dogs* . . . on my foot. It made a mustard mark on my *Ferragamos.*" His expression of mock tragedy, as if he'd described an asteroid falling from the sky and smashing into the Sistine Chapel, made everyone but Rob smile. "But you know in Italy we have a saying: *A ogni uccello il suo nido è bello.* To every bird his own nest is beautiful."

During this rant Massimo had pulled up the agenda on the screen. "OK, to business. Cate is in Atlanta; she asked me to drive the meeting." Rob wondered silently if this was true, but no one objected. "Items number one, two, and three: updates on sales growth initiatives. Who wants to go first?"

Kelly spoke up. "I can give an update on the menu expansion plan. Rob asked me to cover it." Rob was pleased that she started by reminding people this was his idea.

"Everything is on track. We've installed additional refrigeration in all locations so we can expand our offerings of bottled juice, sodas, iced teas—basically the most popular items from what the convenience stores offer so we can compete with them. And we finally got our permits to sell beer and wine in our three biggest cafes. I'm going to visit two distributors tomorrow afternoon to finalize what we'll put on the menu. This will allow us to pick off some of the bar crowd. Last but not least, I signed a partnership with Marathon Caterers to expand our food menu. Should pick up some people looking to grab a bite after work."

"Bravo!" Massimo exclaimed. "All that will also help with the corporate sales program. Speaking of which: James, what's happening with partnership development?" Another brainchild of Rob's, the program was launched to drive more business traffic by signing corporate partners and offering them volume discounts as incentives to their employees. To support this, they'd converted space in their largest locations into conference rooms so on-the-go business teams could hold meetings there during the day.

As James updated the team, Rob frowned inwardly. The presence of the head barista on the executive team seemed particularly unfitting. *He doesn't even have an MBA!*

When James finished, Massimo turned to Rob. "What about you, Rob? Last meeting it sounded like the new marketing tactics were looking promising."

"Why, yes," Rob replied. "We are still doing some analysis—using advanced big data techniques. But an obvious lever to pull for growth—and one that's been overlooked here until recently—is to identify your best customers and figure out how to sell them more of your product. That's the idea behind the Coffee Connoisseurs' Club. We're completing the analyses on our pilot and we should see some results shortly after."

"Excellent!" Massimo said.

He's nothing if not enthusiastic, Rob thought.

"Elena—before we go, do you want to give us an update on the IPO preparation?"

Elena looked serious. "I don't think I need to remind you all that we are in crunch time now. The bankers called me yesterday to express their concern about our quarterly numbers, and I assured them they will not be disappointed. We all need to work hard to not prove me wrong. We have a meeting in two weeks to go over the final preparations, and while we should be in good shape, there is still time for them to pull the plug. Let's make sure that doesn't happen."

Silence fell over the group as they internalized this sobering news. Massimo tried to lighten the mood. "Leave it to a CFO to inject a dose of reality into what was an otherwise lovely morning. All right, everyone, if there are no other agenda items, let's stop talking and get back to work. As they say in the old country, *Belle parole non pascon i gatti.* Fine words don't feed cats."

James gave Kelly a perplexed look, but before he could ask a question, Marcus spoke. "Actually there is one other item Cate asked me to share with you. I know this is disruptive, but we all need to clear our calendars on Monday and Tuesday the week after next. Cate's called for an offsite at the Prescott House for these two days. She wants to get us all on the same page on everything we need to do leading up to the IPO. Two of the board members will be there, and she's bringing along that consultant she's hired to help with our customer insights. She wants us each to give a detailed overview of the programs we're leading, along with projections of the numbers."

Everyone was surprised by this, but their enormous faith in Cate's leadership meant they would follow her anywhere. Everyone except Rob, who was inwardly displeased. *What a waste of time . . . prevents us from getting real work done.* While he was too versed in corporate politics to reveal his distaste for such things, he couldn't resist a small dig at Alex.

"Does she really think someone so new will be able to help at this late juncture?"

Elena wondered silently if Rob, a relative newcomer himself, appreciated the irony of his own remark.

Marcus responded. "I think we've known Cate long enough to trust in her judgment. I'm sure if she's decided it, it's a great idea. Anyway, let's all bring our best selves to the meeting and have a great offsite!"

Typical HR drivel, Rob thought. But as everyone rose to leave, it struck him that the offsite could be a perfect opportunity to impress the board and establish his position once and for all.

5

SMALL DATA

The two researchers stared at the screen for a few moments before Jordan broke the silence.

"Selling more coffee to people who don't drink it—going to be tough. I'm thinking I can create a machine learning algorithm to look for other useful patterns. Lots of big data techniques we can apply here."

"Sounds promising," Alex replied unconvincingly. "But what we need right now is not big data. We need small data."

This got Jordan's attention. In much the same way, Alex imagined, a toddler might get a parent's attention by suggesting that cookies replace broccoli on the dinner menu.

"Small data? What do you mean?" Jordan asked.

"Look . . . I know I have a lot to learn from you about the latest research methods," Alex said. "And there may well be gold to mine from all that data collected over the years. Companies often assume that's the case—that if they have a lot of data it must contain a lot of insight. But insights from data are only as good as the questions asked to generate it. If you ask the wrong questions, data will only yield misleading answers. To ask the right questions, you have to start with small data: observations about a small number of people that help you map out whatever territory you want to explore."

Jordan took a nanosecond to process this idea, then said, "I get it. You're saying, 'Small data before big data.' That's the principle. Cool. So how do we get this small data?"

This was finally a topic where Alex was on more confident footing. "We talk to people. One at a time. And observe them—ideally in their natural habitat."

Over the next hour, Alex explained the details of his approach, including the idea that the most important type of small data they were seeking was an understanding of the jobs Tazza was hired for. He also recapped what he'd learned from Cate, and shared the view that the original jobs Tazza was hired for related to creating a sense of place and belonging. But he emphasized there were many questions still to answer about what was really going on.

As Jordan listened, her enthusiasm grew. Working as a market detective had a particular appeal. "It sounds like we're going on a stakeout," she said. "My fiancé—his name's Mark—will be so jealous."

"That's not a bad way to look at it," Alex observed. "Though we'll be up-front about everything we are doing—not spying on people covertly."

Jordan was pacing now within the narrow confines of her cubicle, as if the overflow of ideas in her head needed a kinetic outlet.

"It's interesting," she said. "This focus on understanding the 'jobs,' as you call them. My Connoisseur Club analysis was focused on our products—what people like or don't like about them. But from what you're describing, it's more like people want community, not coffee."

Alex was impressed. "Why, yes—that's a great way to put it. And you've hit on a key point. When you look at things through the jobs lens, you usually find your products are just part of a broader experience customers are hiring to get a job done."

Alex went on to explain the benefits of viewing and understanding the world through a jobs-centric lens, and how it was preferable to the product-centric lens that's often the default of many companies.

"I get it," said Jordan again. "The principle for that could be 'Avoid the Ptolemy trap.'"

Alex looked confused. "OK, now you've lost me."

Jordan explained. "Ptolemy. Ancient Greek. White beard. Toga. He's the guy who believed the Earth was the center of the universe. That the Sun, Moon, stars, planets—everything revolved around the Earth. Pretty much everyone believed that until Copernicus came along and showed the Sun was at the center and we just rotate around it.

"I got a second major in astronomy for fun," she added, as if this were a perfectly normal thing to do.

"Sounds vaguely familiar," Alex said. "What's the connection?"

"It's just like your two different lenses. Like Ptolemy, companies try to explain the world by putting themselves—or their products—at the center of their models of how things work. But to understand what's really going on, you have to focus on what's really driving things: customers and their jobs to be done."

Alex liked the comparison. "So you're calling that tendency to be self-centered the Ptolemy trap?"

"Almost," Jordan replied. "The trap isn't just having a wrong model. The idea that the Earth was at the center was a sensible one based on what people knew at the time. People were just observing the sky, and everything in it seemed to rotate around them. Then those early astronomers tracked the movements more closely, and there were things they couldn't explain—with more and more puzzles over time. But instead of questioning their model, they kept trying to make small changes to preserve it. Or worse, they ignored the new data entirely.

"That's the Ptolemy trap: ignoring anomalies or inventing elaborate new explanations to preserve a self-centered view of the world. I was starting to fall into it when I was analyzing the purchase habits of the Connoisseurs—assuming the root cause of their behavior was our products. But in that case the anomaly was so big it was obvious—because they weren't even buying our coffee!

"Put another way, it's the idea that you get so wedded to one way of looking at things that, rather than let new information change your worldview, you cling to it even more strongly. Of course *trap* should really be spelled *P-t-r-a-p*, with a silent *P*—since *Ptolemy* has a silent *P* at the beginning." Jordan seemed quite satisfied with this last modification.

Although he'd been hesitant initially, Alex was quickly realizing how good Cate's suggestion to bring Jordan along was.

"I love it. But I'm not yet sold on the silent *P*—might want to think more about the label for your idea."

Jordan grinned. "So when do we start?"

"How does right now sound? Pick you up by the visitors' entrance in ten minutes."

Before Jordan could respond, Alex was out the door. Intrigued and excited, she packed up her laptop and followed a few minutes later.

6

LANGUAGE, METHOD, MINDSET

O nce in the car, they discussed which Tazza location to visit first. Jordan suggested one in a neighboring town about a forty-minute drive away.

"Sales have been dropping at this place faster than any other. And it's one of our largest—makes up about eighteen percent of all our sales. So you have a big share of sales dropping at a faster rate. Not good."

Alex appreciated Jordan's command of the numbers, agreed this made sense, and pulled out of the parking lot toward their destination.

Once they were underway, Jordan took the opportunity to grill Alex further.

"How does a person become a 'market detective'? Is there some special school you attend?"

"As far as I know I invented the term," Alex replied. "So I'm pretty sure there is no school. I do guest lecture occasionally in a friend's business school marketing class. I think he likes that I'm out in the 'real world' and can offer a different perspective to his students."

"What do you teach them?" Jordan asked.

"Well, I usually say that to conduct effective market investigations you need to learn three things: a language, a method, and a mindset.

"The *language* is a kind of new vocabulary that defines what types of small data you are looking for. It's similar to the way practitioners in other fields have their own peculiar language they speak and understand. Doctors talk about acute or chronic conditions, inpatients and outpatients, and every medical specialty has its own language—neurology, cardiology, and so on. Lawyers discuss injunctions, torts, civil actions, and other things opaque to nonlawyers like me. Accountants obsess about cash flows, balance sheets, debits and credits.

"You need a language for understanding customers too—but it needs to be the *right* language so it focuses you on discovering the right things—and at the right level of detail. You're already familiar with one element of this language: the idea of jobs to be done. But there are other things we'll try to understand as well.

"Once you know what you're looking for, you need a *method* for finding it, organizing it, and interpreting it. The method I use is one I've honed over the years, but it's always evolving to some degree. I learn new things from every investigation—and from the work of others."

Jordan was intrigued. "How does the method work?"

"The best way to learn is to see it in action," Alex responded. "Which you will very shortly. There are different ways to apply the method—but today we'll engage people in conversation, ask them questions, and look for clues. Talking directly to customers is often *the* best way to gain real insight—and the most efficient. Yet many people don't make time for it, or they assume you need extensive training. It's true you need to learn *some* things, but honestly *anyone* can with a bit of effort."

Alex paused as he changed lanes to make way for an impatient tailgater, his attention briefly absorbed by the high-speed maneuvering required. The driver glanced blankly at them while he passed, then sped away.

"He was certainly in a hurry," Alex observed. "He's going to miss this lovely scenery we've finally arrived at. Not a bad segue to the last thing you need for these investigations: the right *mindset*. If you don't go into these investigations in the right state of mind, you can miss everything. It's so important, I have a kind of mental checklist I go through before any exercise like this.

"At the top of the list are reminders to be genuinely interested in the people I talk to and to show up with my real self. These are pretty natural for me, but beginners often assume you must be formal and businesslike. In fact the opposite is true. You'd be amazed how much people will share with you when you are genuinely interested in their lives—and willing to share back something about your own.

"The next thing on the mindset checklist is the hardest one—it relates to your Ptolemy Ptrap idea. You have to do your best to clear your mind of preconceptions about what you'll learn—including assumptions or biases related to your current view of the world. This is one reason an outsider like me can sometimes see things that people who have worked in an industry for a long time cannot—because I likely won't have those biases or assumptions."

Jordan nodded thoughtfully. "You know, there's a term for that in Zen Buddhism: they call it having a *beginner's mind*. It means approaching a subject with your mind as a kind of blank slate, even if you're studying it at an advanced level. How about this for the mindset principles: 'Be interested, be authentic, and have a beginner's mind'?"

Alex again felt grateful to have Jordan's help, and said as much as they pulled up to the Tazza cafe in the suburbs.

7

WHY HIRE A CUP OF COFFEE?

This Tazza was as far from a quaint, cozy Italian street-side cafe as Alex could imagine. Housed in one wing of a long-defunct textile factory, the massive interior more resembled a ski lodge, its vaulted ceilings supported by enormous oak beams lined with track lighting. A half-dozen widescreen televisions strewn around the walls streamed a midmorning assortment of reality TV courtrooms, news across the political spectrum, and sports channels. The expansive floor space was covered with a patchwork of small wooden tables leading up to a long, winding coffee bar as the centerpiece.

At eleven in the morning, it was packed, and buzzing with caffeine-infused activity. Alex and Jordan weaved through the maze of people and voices and settled at a table along a side wall where they could see the full expanse of the room.

"Let's sit here for a moment and get our bearings," Alex said.

They settled in and started scanning the room. People were widely dispersed, with a cluster around the food display, a haphazard line leading up to the order counter, and a group watching recaps of a basketball game on two adjacent screens. Off to the right was a large conference room, empty but for one worried-looking, heavyset businessman pacing while talking into his headset. Jordan was struck by the variety of people in the crowd. There were students huddled over books and laptops, a construction crew on break, professionals engaged in rituals of the modern knowledge worker, and two haggard parents studying a tourist map with a trio of unhappy kids bouncing around nearby.

"Who do we talk to first?" Jordan asked, uncertain how they'd go about approaching people.

Alex looked up from his notes. "Think of what we'll be doing over the next few days as building a kind of map of the territory Tazza is operating in. Since we are starting with what you aptly labeled a beginner's mind, it doesn't matter too much who we talk to first. You can overengineer your search for small data in the beginning. Better to just start talking to actual customers—then get more focused as you learn more."

Alex picked up a small envelope he'd brought along and gestured toward the nearest table, where a young woman sat alone reading a thick textbook. "Why don't we start with that table there?" Without waiting for a response, he stood and headed toward the table. It seemed sensible to Jordan to follow along, so she did.

"Hi—I'm Alex," he said as they approached. "This is Jordan. We work for Tazza. We're doing some research on how people feel about the experience here. We'd love to ask you a few questions.

"We can offer you a twenty-dollar Tazza gift certificate for your trouble," he added, clearing up the mystery of the envelope.

The young woman seemed almost grateful for the interruption. "Of course! Happy to help. I love Tazza, I'm here all the time. My name's Amelia."

"Nice to meet you, Amelia. How often do you come here?"

"Every Monday, Wednesday, and Friday, and sometimes on the weekend. Oh, and I came here last Saturday for the open mic night. My friend Julie was singing with her band, the Free Radicals."

"That sounds a little subversive," Alex noted.

Jordan interrupted. "It's not subversive. Free radicals are ionized molecules in chemistry. It's a play on words." She pointed at the open organic chemistry book on the table.

Amelia nodded. "That's right. Julie's my TA for chem class. She plays in her band with a bunch of grad students. I'm premed."

"Got it," Alex said. "So what's special about Monday, Wednesday, Friday?"

"That's when I have chem class. I come here right after it's over. Sometimes before."

"Always by yourself?"

"Usually, though I bump into people I know here some-times. But mostly I'm by myself, which is just as well since I can concentrate on my homework."

"Is that one of the reasons you come here? To get your schoolwork done?"

"Yes."

"Why this place?"

Amelia paused for a moment to reflect. "I guess because it's so convenient and I get a lot done. It's so close to school that I can get here right after the lecture, when everything is still fresh. And it's big enough that you can kind of feel like you are by yourself, even in the midst of all these people. Less chance anyone will notice you or that you'll see some-one you know. I mean, I'm not an antisocial person, it's just that this chem class is really hard. I do like people watching here—it's good when I need a short mental break."

"That makes sense," said Alex. "How did you discover Tazza?"

"Just walked by it one day on my way home from class."

"Any other places you go to get homework done?"

"Sometimes I work in the library, but it's so quiet in there that any little noise breaks my concentration. Plus, I feel like everyone is checking everyone out. It's distracting. It's funny, you'd think the library would be more serious than this coffee shop, but the library always seems like more of a scene. The cafe is much noisier, but it's like all the com-motion creates a kind of white noise in the background that helps me focus.

"I can't work in my apartment. I live with three other roommates in a dorm. There is always the temptation of something fun to do, or else there is some drama going on. But this year I have to be really serious since next year I apply to medical school and my grades have to be good. A couple of times I tried working in one of the empty classrooms, but didn't like that either."

"Why not?"

"It was just *too* quiet. Felt kind of lonely. At least here I'm around people . . . I guess that sounds strange because I just said I don't want to be interacting with people when I work! I suppose I like being alone but *with* other people," she added with a laugh.

Jordan noticed that Alex had not yet asked any questions pertaining to coffee purchases, so she jumped in.

"What are you drinking?" she asked. Amelia's large mug was full and looked untouched.

"Just a large coffee of the day, black. Might go through a couple of these while I'm here. I'm not a big coffee drinker but I figure it's kind of like paying the rent for this table. I know it's a business after all, and I'd feel guilty if I was just taking up space here without buying anything. Sometimes I don't even drink it. I guess I could order a small size, but somehow I feel like I should order a large one as the cost of entry."

"Why not order something you would definitely drink?" Jordan asked.

"Hmm . . . that's a good question. That would make more sense, wouldn't it? Maybe because I like how it smells. Also, something about it reminds me of home—both my parents are big coffee drinkers and maybe the sight and smell of coffee makes me feel more connected to them somehow. They're back in Ohio. Only get to see them on holidays."

Alex picked up again. "Anything about the experience here frustrating for you? Changes that would make it a better experience?"

Amelia thought for a moment. "You know, there is one thing: power outlets! There are only a few scattered around on the walls, and since I get here in late morning all the outlets are always taken. I know where they all are, and if I sit at a table too far away to plug in my laptop, I'm constantly scanning the room waiting for someone to leave one of those prime power-outlet tables. Kind of a pain. Or I just take notes on paper when my battery dies, but then I have to go back and transfer them to my computer later. Also a pain."

"I can relate to that," Alex said. "When traveling I often duck into a cafe to send some emails or work on my computer, and the first thing I do is scout out the outlets. You also mentioned you were here on a Saturday night recently—to hear your friend's band. Why did you choose to come to Tazza that night? Is that what you usually do on Saturdays?"

"Never. And probably wouldn't do it again. I was just here to support Julie. My friend Candace says I only went so Julie would give me a better grade, but if she knew anything about how organic chem class works, she'd know that is impossible. I like Julie and think we'll be friends after this class is over."

"Why wouldn't you do it again?" Alex asked.

"The whole scene was kind of lame," Amelia answered. "Not much of a crowd. And mostly older people. I mean . . . there's nothing wrong with older people. No offense."

"None taken," Alex assured her.

"Also, Julie's band seemed to be having fun but they weren't that good. Good thing they all have fallback careers."

"What do you like to do on Saturday nights?"

"Go out with my friends. Go to clubs, dance. I love live music as well, but it has to be good music. The main thing is being with my friends. But I'm single, so it's not a bad thing if there are new people to meet too, you know? And I have so little free time with my course load, so when I do go out I have to make it count."

They continued in this fashion for some time, filling in further details of her background and current life, including what kinds of activities and beverages she enjoyed. Jordan was struck by how open Amelia was to speaking to them, even about quite personal details, and by how long it lasted—nearly forty-five minutes. Despite this, the conversation seemed to meander quite a bit, leaving Jordan uncertain how much useful information they'd learned.

When they wrapped up, they thanked Amelia for her time and left the promised gift certificate. As they withdrew Jordan shared her concerns.

"That was interesting, but I'm not sure we learned much."

Alex looked surprised. "On the contrary—this was a great step forward." He leaned forward and with a melodramatic air said, "I have no doubt you will be running Tazza—and probably the world—before long . . . but in this case *you see, but you do not observe.*"

"Is that Yoda? Sounds like Yoda."

"No. Sherlock Holmes. From 'A Scandal in Bohemia.'"

Jordan couldn't help grinning as she followed him back to their home-base table. This was way more fun than making charts for Rob.

8

JOB SPEC

As soon as they sat down, Alex explained. "I confess I'm a Sherlock Holmes nut. I read the complete works of Arthur Conan Doyle so many times when I was a kid that I have a habit of quoting him at odd moments. It annoys my wife, but she puts up with it. All I meant by 'seeing but not observing' is that we are looking at what Amelia told us through different lenses—so we see different things."

Alex continued talking while he opened his notebook and tore out a blank page. "It's like when I look at your screens full of numbers and charts: I can scarcely make any sense of it—but to you it's full of meaning. My lens for that type of data—big data—is pretty blurry. When it comes to small data my lens is better. The good news is anyone can learn it."

"I'd love to learn," Jordan said. "Where do we start?"

Alex responded by scribbling something on the page he'd torn out and placing it on the table between them.

JOB SPEC: Amelia

Questions	Specs

"Recall the three things you need for a proper market investigation: a language, a method, and a mindset. I've described the most important part of the language: the jobs people are trying to get done. If you wanted to hire for a job, what would you need? You'd need a description of that job—a *job spec*. That's what we'll create for Amelia—and by doing this you'll learn the rest of the language. The method should start making sense too."

Alex turned the paper around so Jordan could read it more clearly. "I saw you were taking detailed notes during our conversation. What's the first topic we covered with Amelia?"

Jordan examined her notes. "You first asked her about how often she came here—time of day, who she was with— that sort of thing."

"Right." Alex wrote a question in the Questions column: "What circumstance are you in?"

Alex explained. "We always want to understand the *circumstance* someone is in when trying to get specific jobs done. This is the next element of our language, and answering this question is the first step in our method. Lots of things could define a person's circumstances; some are situational, like what time of day it is, who you are with, what else you are doing, where you are. I think of these as *zoom in* factors, which are relatively narrow in time and space. Then there are broader, *zoom out* factors, like where you are in your life, what your beliefs are, your family or financial status—these are things that may change, but more slowly."

Jordan saw the relevance immediately. "So for Amelia the zoom in variables are things like on the way to/from chem class, in the morning, by herself. The zoom out variables are things like in college, junior year, getting ready to apply for medical school. Actually she also said she came to Tazza on a Saturday night too. Is that a different zoom in circumstance?"

"For sure. Let's write all that in our job spec."

Jordan did so, then turned it around to show Alex.

JOB SPEC: Amelia

Questions	Specs
1. What **circumstance** are you in?	**Zoom in:** • Late morning OR • Saturday night • After class • With friends • Weekdays • Alone **Zoom out:** • Junior year of college • Pre-med • Single, female, extended family in another state • Has student loans/financial aid

Alex continued. "Once you've discovered a customer's circumstances, you have a choice about how broadly or narrowly to define the circumstances of interest for your investigation. It's like selecting the field of vision for where to focus our lens; it can be a very narrow slice of someone's life and experience, or much broader. But for now we just want to capture both the zoom in and zoom out aspects for Amelia."

Before Alex could comment further, Jordan pressed forward. "The next thing we got into was why Amelia came to Tazza. That must relate to the jobs she was trying to get done."

"Indeed. The second question is 'What jobs are you trying to get done?'" Alex said as he added it to the Questions column. "In her specific circumstances, of course. What did we learn about Amelia's jobs?"

Jordan consulted her notes again. "She came to Tazza to do her homework. You asked a follow-up question about that, and she said that's the main reason she comes here after class, except for one time when she came on a weekend night to hear her friend's band. So I guess those would be two different jobs: 'get schoolwork done' and 'have fun with my friends' or 'be entertained' or something like that. Does that mean there are different jobs depending on the circumstance?"

Alex could tell the processing speed of Jordan's brain was ultrafast, as she had already accelerated past the slow pace of his explanations and was seeing their implications.

"Yes," he said. "That's why it's so important to understand the circumstance. The same person might hire the same solution for different jobs depending on the circumstance. Or a solution might be great in one circumstance, but terrible in another. This leads us to the third question."

Alex wrote down this question beneath the first two: "What do you hire to get those jobs done, and why?"

"OK," he said, "that's a bit of a cheat since that 'why' makes it two questions. But you'll see they are closely related. What did we learn about this?"

"Well, she hires Tazza of course," Jordan said. "But she also mentioned the library and her dorm, and how it was hard to work there. Oh, and an empty classroom—also a bad solution. She seemed pretty happy with Tazza for the job of getting her schoolwork done. Not so much for the Saturday-night jobs. For that she preferred clubs or bars—or some kind of event like concerts."

"Excellent," said Alex. "You've illustrated two key aspects of the method there. The first is that it helps us understand how people define a quality solution for jobs in different circumstances. For job number one—'get schoolwork done'—Amelia *liked* having few people she knows at Tazza because there are fewer distractions. But for job number two—'connect with friends'—the opposite is true."

"Right," Jordan interjected. "She said the library is too quiet, and so any little noise breaks her concentration. Also, there are people checking everyone out—another distraction. Her dorm room sounds like a nonstarter—just too much chaos with people coming and going, interrupting her, grabbing her attention. But Tazza worked."

Alex nodded and continued. "The second thing probing on solutions helps us to understand is the *real competition* for Tazza," he said, "which again depends on the job and circumstance. For job number one, the competition is the library and dorm room, and likely other cafes. For job number two, it's bars and clubs and concerts."

"This is fascinating," Jordan observed. "It's like Tazza is competing in two different markets at once."

"And likely more than two," Alex agreed. "Eventually we'll map all these out—once we have more small data about other types of customers. But there was even more we learned about how she defines quality. What specifically about Tazza did she like?"

"She liked that it's so spacious," Jordan answered. "It's big enough to be lost in the crowd, unnoticed. She liked the buzz of the background noise—said it's like white noise that helps her concentrate. So I guess for her *quality* means things like 'minimal distractions from noise or other people,' 'a place where I'm unlikely to be noticed,' which might relate to the size of the place—that sort of thing. But she doesn't like *no* noise or *no* people—she likes some of both to be in the right state of mind for studying."

"Good," said Alex. "That raises another point. Understanding how she defines quality means we understand the dimensions of quality—for example ambient noise level in this case—and what she views as good, bad, or great on those dimensions. This is *so* important because it helps us understand where there are opportunities to better solve for the jobs—what I refer to as the *help wanted* signs. Which leads us to the last question."

Alex wrote at the bottom of the sheet, "What are the help wanted signs?"

Jordan was already answering the question. "This is where you asked her how things could be improved, right? She seemed pretty satisfied overall. She did mention there were not enough power outlets—I can *definitely* relate to that. Also, there was that strange thing about buying coffee even though she didn't always drink it. Said she felt obligated— it's like 'paying the rent' for the table. But the coffee did make her feel connected to her family. Wait—could that be another job? 'Stay connected to my family when I'm away from home.' She's actually hiring Tazza and the coffee for that, even though it's not a great solution."

"Great—let's add that job to our job spec. You could consider her coffee purchase a workaround. This is a solution someone just improvises because the job is really important but there is no good solution available. Seeing one is usually a sign of a great business opportunity, because it reveals an important job with no adequate solution."

Jordan displayed her cup of coffee and pointed to the cardboard sleeve surrounding it. "Here's an example of that: Back in the dark ages before we had these things to prevent our fingers from getting too hot, people would just nest two cups together to achieve the same result. Then someone had the idea for these little sleeves—work just as well and save paper. It probably funded the yacht they are now sailing around their own private island."

"And the opportunity was in front of our noses all that time," Alex agreed. "Literally—every time we took a sip. Anyway, that's it—those four questions form the backbone of the method we're using. They frame all the types of information we are looking for, listed at the right. Once you understand all these terms, you officially speak the language as well. We capture it all in the job spec for each person we talk to."

All of this made sense to Jordan, and she rapidly filled in the rest of the job spec.

"One thing I'm struck by is how much the little details of the Tazza experience matter to Amelia," she said. "You can see that in all these details in the job spec. I'm mixing metaphors here, but it's like the spec defines the shape of a lock, and the Tazza experience is the key that fits it perfectly."

"Great observation—that's almost always the case," agreed Alex. "Usually the products we love the most are those that match the requirements of our job specs—right down to the smallest details. That's why all the elements of our language are important—they give us a way to capture the richness of detail we need. Ignoring these details is a good way to lose customers. Holmes said it best: 'It has long been an axiom of mine that the little things are infinitely the most important.' From the story 'A Case of Identity.'"

"Nice," said Jordan, still amused by Alex's referential habit. "One thing I don't understand though—you say these four questions are the backbone of the method. But you never actually asked Amelia any of those questions. Why not?"

JOB SPEC: Amelia

Questions	Specs
1. What **circumstance** are you in?	**Zoom in:** • Late morning OR • Saturday night • After class • With friends • Weekdays • Alone **Zoom out:** • Junior year of college • Pre-med • Single, female, extended family in another state • Has student loans/financial aid
2. **What jobs** are you trying to get done?	**Functional, social, emotional jobs** • Get schoolwork done • Spend time with friends • Be entertained • Feel connected to family
3. What do you **hire** to get those jobs done, and **why**?	**Current solutions/Workarounds** • Tazza • Library/Dorm • Bar/club/concert **Definition of "quality"** • No distractions • Background "white noise" • Large space/big enough to be anonymous/hide in the crowd • Access to power for laptop • Not far from dorm/class
4. What are the **"help wanted"** signs?	• More access to power • New people to meet • Better quality music

"Well, we have to use language she would understand—and she doesn't know this somewhat strange vocabulary of ours. Think of the four questions as a guide to the information we are trying to gather—more fundamental than the techniques we use to answer them. Some techniques are better than others, of course. My personal favorite is what we've just done—talking to customers directly. But you can get useful info in lots of ways—interviews, focus groups, observation, even reinterpreting research you've already done. As long as you're asking the right questions. I bet even all those modern big data methods you could teach me—assuming I'm capable of learning them—a big assumption—could help answer them."

Jordan seemed to be processing again, then said, "So the principle could be *The questions you ask are not the questions you seek to answer.*"

"OK, that *definitely* sounds like Yoda," Alex observed. Somehow this pleased Jordan.

"I can see how all these pieces fit together," she said.

"That's great," said Alex. "Because you're leading the next interview."

Before Jordan could protest, Alex set out toward another table, whose occupants looked about as different from Amelia as Jordan could imagine.

9

NEW TERRITORY

T he three gray-haired men seated at the table Alex and
Jordan approached appeared to be arguing over what
looked like a game with oversize, domino-like tiles inscribed
with Chinese characters.

"This never happened when Barb was here," complained
the lone occupant on one side of the table. He picked up a
piece from a pile at the center of the board and placed it with
an air of disgust onto a small rack in front of him.

"Just play, Gerald," rejoined the man seated directly opposite him. "You're only mad because you're losing for the
fifth time this week and your chance of winning this month's
challenge is basically zero."

"We said this match wasn't going to count toward our
rankings," argued Gerald.

"Wrong. You're thinking of Tuesday's game at O'Sullivan's. And that was because you spilled ketchup on the board."

To Jordan's surprise, Alex interrupted, introduced them both, and explained their objectives. To her greater surprise, the three men agreed to speak to them. Gerald even seemed eager to have them join.

"Please have a seat," said Gerald. "You're just in time: you've saved me from an embarrassing loss to the worst mahjong player east of the Mississippi. I'm Gerald. This is Al, and this is Chuck. Supposedly they are my friends."

As they shook hands and shifted to make room around the table, Al said, "They've discovered the world is round, Gerald. Everything is east of the Mississippi if you travel far enough."

"Good to know."

Well, here goes nothing, Jordan thought, and jumped in. "Thanks so much for taking some time to speak to us. I see you're playing mahjong. Are you missing someone? I know it's not usually played with three people."

Alex gave Jordan a raised eyebrow. She responded with a shrug and said, "I like games."

"Why, yes . . . we used to be a foursome," answered Chuck. "But sadly our friend Barb is no longer with us."

Before anyone could offer condolences, Gerald added, "Don't worry—she's not dead. She just doesn't like coming here anymore."

"Yeah, she prefers the country club now—with all her fancier friends," added Chuck. "Plus, there are more single men there." He gave Gerald a meaningful look.

"You're just jealous, you know I was her favorite," Gerald responded.

"In your dreams, old man," said Chuck, but he smiled and patted Gerald on the arm. It was clear they were all good friends and giving one another a hard time was part of their routine.

The pace and unpredictability of their dialogue made Jordan appreciate the role of the job spec as a guide to orient these conversations. The fate of Barb seemed worth following up on, but she decided to defer that and instead probe on the first of the four questions: *What circumstance are you in?*

"So how often do you come here?" she asked. "And are you always together?"

"Oh yes, we've known each other since ancient times," said Chuck.

"Back before the discovery of electricity," added Gerald.

"Before they discovered fire, in Gerald's case," said Al.

Gerald rolled his eyes. "We grew up together. Same neighborhood, same schools, played on the same football team—just in the next town over. We all drifted around the world in our different jobs but ended up back here after we retired."

"We're here most afternoons during the week, usually around lunchtime," added Al.

"Do you always sit at this same table? Always mahjong?" Jordan asked.

Chuck frowned and said, "We *prefer* to sit at this table. It's the perfect size and shape for playing games. But we don't always get it. These days it's often taken by some self-important yuppie blathering on his cell phone and staring at his computer screen like he's in a trance."

To emphasize his point, Chuck gestured to a man a few tables away who appeared to be talking to the thin air, but was in fact speaking into a small white headset dangling from his ear.

Al explained, "This used to always be our table. People would leave it open for us. Or our favorite barista would protect it for us so it would be available when we got here. But she left a few months ago. Now we have to fend for ourselves."

"She still works at Tazza," Chuck added. "Went on to bigger and better things, I guess. Good for her of course. And no, we don't always play the same game. Switches every month. This is Mahjong Month. Next month we'll play poker, which is great because Gerald is rich and I need money to get my car repaired."

"No amount of money is enough to save that piece of junk," countered Gerald.

Chuck leaned toward Jordan and whispered, "That's actual jealousy."

Jordan again appreciated the value of having the job spec to guide these conversations . . . it would be easy to get off track without it. She glanced at her notebook and decided to move to the next topic: *What jobs are you trying to get done?*

"So why do you like coming here so much?" she asked.

Chuck answered first. "We can't afford a country club. Well, Al and I can't afford it. Gerald could buy everyone in the cafe memberships at a country club. But we'd still probably come to Tazza. We just like it. Feels like home to us. We've been coming here for years."

Gerald piled on. "You might not realize this because you're so young, but when you get to be our age, it's easy to isolate yourself. Have to make an effort to stay connected to people. We're all widowers—makes it harder. Having a regular place to go and something to do there gives us all a reason to get out of the house."

"I can relate to that," said Jordan. "I mean not the widower part . . . it's just that when I first moved to the area, I felt pretty isolated too. Then I started hanging out at Tazza—the one in the North End—almost every day. I'd see the same faces, the same routines, hear the same sounds. Before long I felt more at home too. Made me feel like I was connected to a place, to a community. Less alone."

They all seemed to appreciate this small moment of self-revelation. Jordan decided to move to the next topic. "So what makes this place seem like home?" *What do you hire to get these jobs done today, and why?*

Al jumped in. "The people, for starters. Familiar faces. Like Gerald said, we've known each other a long time. We know a lot of the regulars, and the staff is always real friendly, though we are just getting to know the new folks."

"Also, we can watch TV while we wait for Gerald to play his turn," Chuck added. "Lots of time spent waiting for that."

Chuck again leaned over and whispered to Jordan, "Gerald is terrible at games. World-class lawyer in his day—that's how he got so rich. But just terrible at games."

Gerald shot Chuck a harsh look but didn't respond to the dig. "It's also nice that the place is so big, so you don't feel guilty for taking up too much space," he added.

Jordan pressed on in search of other things the group might be hiring for. "Are there other places you go to get that same feeling of community and connection?"

"O'Sullivan's," Al answered. "It's a bar down the street—but that doesn't open until five o'clock. We're not exactly night owls—we all go to bed pretty early—so it's not ideal. Plus, it's a pretty small space."

"And the tables are sticky," added Chuck. "Not good for cards."

"I visit my kids sometimes, too, and my grandkids," Gerald said. "Love doing that, but it's different somehow. And when I play games with the grandkids I feel like I have to let them win."

Chuck was about to make another sarcastic comment, but Gerald shot a look that dissuaded him.

"Do you all live around here?" Jordan asked. "Is the location of Tazza or O'Sullivan's important?"

"For sure. We can all walk here in ten minutes or less. Otherwise would be hard to meet up so often."

Glancing one more time at her notes, Jordan decided to move on to the last question. "Anything we could do to make the experience here better? What would make it an even more appealing place to come?" *What are the help wanted signs?*

Gerald answered without a beat. "More single people over the age of seventy."

"Or sixty," Al countered. "Also, what about some sort of table guarantee? So we always get this same table—kind of like a dedicated parking spot."

Chuck looked thoughtful for a moment, then said, "You know, I worked in marketing for many years. One piece of advice I'd have for you is don't change things so much. Seems like lately there's always some new program or gimmick they're rolling out. A while back I got a notice I was invited to be a member of some rewards program—the Connoisseurs' Club or something like that. But guess what? I don't drink coffee. Don't get me wrong, I love free stuff. But it made me feel like Tazza doesn't actually know me that well—that's the opposite of how it always made me feel in the past."

"Those are all great ideas," Jordan said. "Though I'm not sure we can guarantee a better singles scene. That reminds me: Why do you think Barb left?"

"To be honest, I don't think any of us really knows," answered Al. "She loved it here as much as anyone. Was a bit of a shock to all of us. We assumed she just needed a change, or maybe she wanted to hang out with her girlfriends more. We all sure miss her. We still think she might come back someday."

Jordan felt they'd learned a lot and moved to wrap things up. "Well, thank you all so much for spending the time."

Alex finally spoke: "One other question—do you think Barb would mind if we spoke to her? We're trying to understand why people left Tazza—and maybe we can even convince some of them to come back." Alex tried not to look at Gerald when he said this.

Gerald perked up. "Of course! I'll write down her email address for you. I'm sure she'd be happy to speak to you. Just tell her Gerald sent you. Make sure you say that—*Gerald sent you.*"

"Will do," responded Alex. He pulled out a twenty-dollar gift certificate for each of the three, but as he extended one to Gerald, Chuck grabbed it and said, "I'll take his."

10

MORE CLUES

A s they stepped away from the three friends' table Alex whispered to Jordan, "That was fantastic! Perfectly executed. You're a natural. Really well done."

"Thanks, Alex! It was easier than I thought it would be—and fun. Seems like we learned a lot but need time to process it all. Should we fill out another job spec for the three friends?"

"For sure," said Alex. "But first I suggest we do a couple more interviews—before the workday ends. That way we'll have a broader sample of small data to review tomorrow."

"OK. Who's next? How do you pick which people to talk to?"

"Good question. Since we're just starting to create our map, it's best to find different types of people so we can sample as much of the territory as possible. That's why we went from Amelia to the three old friends."

"So the principle could be 'Sample extremes,'" said Jordan. "At least in the beginning."

"I like it. Why don't I lead this next interview? That reminds me of another good practice: do these interviews with two people if you can. One person will always notice things the other won't. Plus, you can trade off so each person stays fresh."

Alex scanned the room for their next destination. "I think I see our next extreme," he said. "Let's go."

Jordan saw that Alex was headed directly toward the businessperson Chuck had gestured at earlier as evidence of Tazza's decline. *Good choice*, she thought as she followed behind.

In contrast to the previous people they'd approached, the man looked decidedly irritated by their interruption. But Alex's introduction was gracious, and the man, whose name was Mike, agreed to speak to them.

"Just for a few minutes," he emphasized, looking at his watch. "I could use a mental break. Working on a big deal here." Jordan wondered if one of his jobs to be done was to have his ego bolstered by people interested in asking him questions, but figured that could only be a good thing.

"Thanks, Mike," said Alex. "We understand you're busy and we'll be very efficient."

As in the previous two conversations, Alex started by probing into the man's circumstances. "Do you live in the area?"

"No," replied Mike. "I live in Florida. In town for a convention at the hotel down the street. That's where I'm staying."

"What kind of convention?" Alex asked.

"Medical sales conference. Big boondoggle. I was the top salesman in the Southeast region last year—for the past three years actually—so I get a free trip to this conference. Of course there are prospective clients here too, so it's a great hunting ground. Gotta keep the pipeline filled, you know?"

"I do indeed," replied Alex. "Why did you come to this cafe today?"

"Hotel recommended it. Just needed a place to work for the afternoon. Hate to disappoint you, but it wasn't some complex decision. Didn't really matter to me where I went as long as there was Wi-Fi and coffee."

"Why not just work in the hotel? In the lobby area?"

"Too many people I know there. Too many interruptions. People wanting advice, or just wanting a bit of the ol' Mike magic to rub off on them."

"I see. Why not just work in your room?"

"You're kidding, right? Too depressing. And I'm not a total loser. I like working around other people even if I never talk to them."

"Got it. What kind of work do you do when you come to this cafe?"

"Mostly working the pipeline. Do some calls—new leads or early-stage discussions. And update info in my spreadsheets."

"Do you have meetings here? Or would you consider it?"

"No. Not my kind of place for that. Have to maintain my brand, you know? I'm a premium product. Only meet clients at high-end restaurants, or at executive conference rooms. I did try one of those shared workspace places once that are becoming all the rage, but it was terrible. So unprofessional. People riding skateboards in the halls. Pets everywhere. Actually saw a puppy jump on a conference table and knock over a pitcher of water on a live projector."

"I can see how that would be distracting," Alex observed. "They have a conference room space you can rent here at Tazza—it just opened and they are trying to appeal to business customers like yourself. Why not use that?"

"Yeah, I saw that. Just doesn't meet my standards. Maybe works for the local PTA or a small business. I doubt big company execs would use it."

"I see. Anything that we could do to make the experience better for your purposes of getting work done?"

"I dunno. Not really. Maybe turn the music down? Or reduce the foot traffic. Hard to hear my calls sometimes, you know?"

As if on cue, Mike's phone rang. "Look man, I have to take this. Nice chatting with you. Good luck."

Alex mouthed a silent thank-you and he and Jordan regrouped at their home-base table.

"Wow," Jordan said. "He was really something."

Alex smiled. "Yes. You meet a diverse cast of characters in this line of work. But we learned a lot from him—we are definitely sampling extremes. Let's do one more interview before we call it a day. Why don't you choose the next one, and you can lead it?"

"OK." Jordan did a full visual sweep of the room before settling on two women in workout gear engaged in quiet conversation off in a corner. "There," she said. "Let's go talk to them."

After making their introductions and again being invited to have a seat, Jordan launched into the interview flow she'd become familiar with. They learned the women had become friends while taking a class at the yoga studio next door and had a post-workout tradition of going for coffee at Tazza. Olivia was a thirty-something stay-at-home mom with two young kids, and Maggie was a single lawyer in her late twenties. Both lived within walking distance of the cafe, and both clearly hired Tazza for the primary job of connecting with friends.

But Jordan discovered other insights as she continued her questioning.

"Maggie—you mentioned this is the second time you've come here today, and the first was early morning. Can you describe your experience earlier today?"

"Sure. Every morning—Monday through Friday, as long as I'm not traveling for work—I drop by Tazza right when it opens at six a.m. just to pick up a large black coffee—French roast—on my way to the office. I'd say I'm only here for about five minutes, so it's really just to fuel up with some caffeine for the morning. To be honest, the work I do as a new associate in a law firm is not exactly a recipe for staying wide awake. And I'm often up late working the night before . . . so I don't know what I'd do without this pick-me-up."

"Why do you come here?" Jordan asked. "Don't they have coffee at work?"

"You know, that's a great question," Maggie said. "Yes, they do. And my dad always tells me I'm insane because I could get a free coffee if I just waited another twenty minutes. He thinks I'm wasting money. He even sent me a spreadsheet once in which he calculated the long-term value of all the money I spend each month on coffee if I instead invested it in a retirement fund. I ignored him."

Alex refrained from commenting that this seemed a very reasonable thing for her dad to do. He really was getting old.

"Why is that?" Jordan asked. "Was it not that much money?"

"Oh no—quite the contrary. It was a large number—so large, I'm embarrassed to tell you what it was. But I earn a good income at my job, and I'm careful to save, so I feel pretty good about that."

"So why come here? Is the coffee a lot better?"

Maggie laughed. "Actually, we have Tazza coffee at work too. I guess it's because it's part of my routine. Somehow coming here first thing in the day helps to clear my mind— it's like hitting the reset button. It's a little bit of a walk, and I like that too—but not so far that it takes up too much time. When I'm here I always see a few familiar faces. I might chat with them for a few minutes. It's kind of a morning ritual, you know? It helps me feel grounded in the midst of what is usually an insanely hard workweek. I feel like if I just went straight to work, I'd never be able to get the feeling of a reset. I definitely don't get that when I get home late at night because I'm too tired."

"I can relate to that," said Jordan. "What about you, Olivia? It's clearly important for both of you to spend time catching up with each other, but are there other things you feel like you get out of coming to Tazza just after your yoga class?"

"Oh yes," Olivia replied. "I get a break! I have two boys under the age of ten. Love being their mom. They are so precious. But they are a handful! It takes a huge amount of energy—and, if I may say so, ingenuity—just to get them out of bed, fed, clothed—with their shirts facing in the right direction—and to school on time. I'm worn out by then, even though the day has just started. Yoga reinvigorates me, and then having the chance to catch up with Maggie is so wonderful. I get to interact with an adult! And live a bit vicariously through her, I should add."

Jordan felt more confident leading this conversation, and continued to probe on the dimensions of the job spec until she felt it was complete. After she and Alex wrapped up, they thanked the two women, packed up their things, and headed to the exit.

Jordan felt exhilarated, but exhausted. "It does take a lot of energy, leading these interviews," she observed. "It's like you're having to keep track of two conversations at once: the one with the people you're speaking to, and the one in your head where you keep track of what insights you've discovered and what you still need to understand."

"I feel the same way," said Alex. "That's why it's important to have a method you trust, so you can capture what you need and have it available for the next step in our investigation."

"Which is?" Jordan asked.

"Let's cover that tomorrow," Alex replied. "I suggest we both get some rest tonight. We'll need all our mental faculties to make progress as fast as we need to. The clock is ticking, and Cate is counting on us."

11

PATTERNS

The next morning Alex and Jordan met back at Tazza headquarters. After fueling up from the coffee cold-brew tap in the common area, they settled into an empty conference room for the day. The room was one of several designed for brainstorming and team problem-solving, with all of its walls doubling as whiteboards.

"My daughter would love this," Alex observed. "Walls you can write on."

"Might start a bad habit though," Jordan said. "Once in my apartment I was so absorbed in a math problem I wrote some equations on our living room walls. Mostly scrubbed them off—but if you look hard you can still see them. If Mark—he's my fiancé—ever noticed he'd be alarmed. He's kind of a neat freak."

"Let's hope that doesn't happen. Anyway, should we start by completing the rest of the job specs from yesterday?"

"Already done," Jordan responded, pulling a stack of papers from her backpack. "I filled the rest in last night. Also created a template for it on my computer so we can create them digitally from now on."

"Wow—that's great, Jordan. Much appreciated."

"No big deal. Was pretty basic, really. I even had time to read this," she said, extracting a book from her backpack. "I figured if there *was* ever a class on being a market detective, this would be on the syllabus. Found it in a used bookstore on my way home last night."

Alex saw that she was holding a weathered copy of *The Adventures of Sherlock Holmes*.

"Ha! Even better," he said, once again impressed by the sheer processing power of Jordan's mind. "That's one of my all-time favorites. We'll have to compare notes when we have a moment."

"It's a plan. Anyway, how do we make sense of all this? What's the next step in the process?"

Alex grabbed a marker and went to the nearest wall. "Before we go there, let's recap where we've been so far. We started this work because there was a market mystery to solve. A case to crack. Before we met, we'd each already started hypothesizing about what was going on—just from different perspectives. That's always the first step: describing the basic features of the case, even if you don't have too much info. That way you're clear on what problem you're trying to solve. It also helps with pattern recognition, as over time you develop a mental library of similar cases you can draw from."

"Wait—that reminds me of something Holmes said," Jordan responded, picking up her book and leafing through it hurriedly, looking for a quote. "Here it is: 'As a rule, when I have heard some slight indication of the course of events, I am able to guide myself by the thousands of other similar cases which occur to my memory.' From the story 'The Red Headed League.'"

"Nice. You're already getting the hang of dropping Sherlock Holmes references," Alex said with a laugh. "It's spot on, though. At the beginning of a case, you likely only have some basic facts about the situation, so the first step is to combine those facts with your previous experience to *imagine* what might be going on. That's why I call this first step 'Imagine.' It's where you sketch out your ingoing understanding of the case and whatever initial hypotheses you might have about what's going on."

Alex wrote this on the whiteboard inside a large arrow representing the initial step.

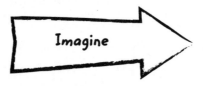

"Doesn't that conflict with the idea of going into the investigation with a beginner's mind?" Jordan asked.

"It's a careful balance you have to strike," Alex responded. "You need *some* initial hypotheses, or you won't know where to begin. But you must remember they are just that: initial hypotheses—and be prepared to adapt them, or even throw them out, as soon as you start talking to customers.

"That brings me to the second step: Investigate. This is where you spend most of your time—out in the world, talking to people, observing, looking for clues. We started this yesterday, and we'll do much more of this over the next week. As you investigate, you want to capture and organize what you learn—using tools like the job spec—in a form that's useful for the third step: Interpret."

Alex built out the picture on the whiteboard.

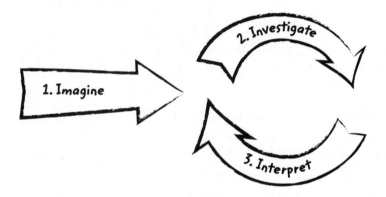

"In practice, steps two and three are not really linear, but kind of a loop. You investigate, then you interpret the information you gathered, then that might influence what you investigate next, and so on. So I draw it as a cycle like this. Gradually, with a few loops, what's happening starts to come into focus."

Before he could comment further, Jordan jumped up and started building on his picture.

"I just noticed something . . . ," she said. "One of my old professors loved finding simple pictures to represent ideas—and I picked up his habit. Your picture kind of looks like a magnifying glass. That first step is the handle, which you hold to point it in the direction of the case you're trying to crack. The loop is like the lens you look through, and as you cycle through the two steps in the loop the picture of what's going on comes into focus. What do you think?"

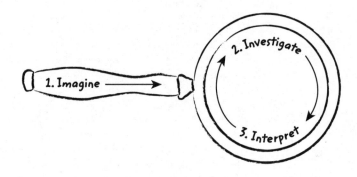

"Brilliant!" Alex replied. "What's a detective without a magnifying glass? Nothing more iconic in mystery stories than that. There's one other thing we need in the picture, though—it's what goes inside the lens. It's the thing we're trying to bring into focus—and the answer to the question you asked earlier about how we make sense of what's going on."

Alex drew a small grid inside the lens.

"What's that?" Jordan asked.

"I call it a *market map*. It's *the* key tool for understanding why we get hired—and why we get fired. It will help us understand where we play today, who we compete with,

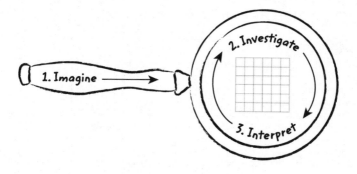

and why we win or lose. And it will give us—and more importantly, the Tazza leadership team—ideas for what to do next.

"It belongs in the center of your lens, because all our cycles of investigation and interpretation will bring the market map into sharper focus. But we already know enough to create an initial one. So that's what we'll do next."

Alex moved to a blank wall and drew a much larger version of the grid.

"First thing you need on any map is coordinates—like latitude and longitude. For market maps, latitude is the jobs people are trying to get done, and longitude is the circumstance in which they have those jobs.

"Every box in this matrix is a potential place Tazza could play—as defined by the intersection of a job and a circumstance. Let's start to fill it in and you'll see how it works. What job specs do we have from our conversations yesterday?"

Jordan spread them out on the table. "We have four—maybe five—different profiles. Mike the businessman, Amelia the college student, the three old friends, and then Maggie and Olivia, who we spoke to last. I think those two

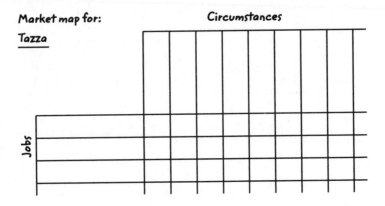

women are really two different profiles since they had some-what different jobs and circumstances—so I did them sepa-rately. If you agree, that's five."

"I do agree," Alex said. "Who should we start with?"

Jordan picked up a profile. "How about Amelia the college student? Seems like a pretty straightforward one to understand."

"Great," Alex responded. "Now here's a key thing about market maps: many companies would be tempted to put Amelia in a single segment. But for her there are at least two, each corresponding to one of the circumstances we identi-fied in which she hired Tazza."

To illustrate this, Alex filled in the first two Circumstance columns with "Late morning" and "Saturday night."

"I'm labeling those two circumstances by the time of day and week, but in reality there are several other variables that define them. *Late morning*, for example, is just shorthand for that cluster of factors from the job spec: late morning, weekdays, after class, by herself. Same for *Saturday night*.

Now let's fill in the jobs we identified for Amelia. Can you read those off for me please?"

"We have five jobs," Jordan said. "Get schoolwork done, spend time with friends, be entertained, feel connected to family, meet new people."

Alex wrote these in the Jobs rows, then continued. "The last thing we do is mark the boxes where we've learned a customer's job and circumstance intersect. I use a check mark to indicate the job is well satisfied by the solution of interest—in this case, Tazza. I mark it with an X if a customer has that job in that circumstance, but there are big help wanted signs."

Alex quickly populated the full map for Amelia.

Market map for: Tazza   **Circumstances**

Jobs		Amelia— Late morning	Amelia— Saturday night			
	Get schoolwork done	✓				
	Feel connected with family	X				
	Connect with friends		X			
	Be entertained		X			
	Meet new people		X			

"Already we can see some useful insights," said Alex. "The first is that the market for Amelia is really two separate markets—each corresponding to one of the different circumstances in which she hired Tazza. That's consistent with what we learned from her: that there are different competitors for each of those markets, and different ways that Amelia defines *quality* for what a good solution is. What else do you see?"

Jordan studied the map for a moment. "Well, Tazza is clearly a great fit for the job 'get schoolwork done.' For all the rest, it's either a mediocre or a bad solution. Or maybe that means there's an opportunity to innovate and get it right."

"Yeah, it could go either way," said Alex. "The map doesn't make recommendations. It just reveals patterns. If Tazza is a bad solution for a job in a particular circumstance, it could mean we should innovate to make it better; or it could mean that we shouldn't be worrying about that segment. Let's fill in the rest and see what we have."

Over the next hour Jordan and Alex worked to populate the rest of the map. Along the way, they noticed some jobs had similar themes and decided to use these to group the jobs into four categories: get work done, connect, be entertained, and maintain well-being. When it was complete, they stepped back to view the results.

"There we have it," said Alex. "Based on a handful of interviews, our first view of where Tazza plays today, across a number of jobs and circumstances—the first function of a market map. If we combine that with the information in our job specs, we also have an initial view of who we are competing with in these different squares, and some sense of why we win or lose.

Market map for:

Tazza

Circumstances

Jobs	Amelia—Late morning	Amelia—Saturday night	Mike—Mobile worker	The 3 Friends—Retired	Maggie—Early morning	Maggie—After workout	Olivia—After workout
Get work done—computer	✓		✗				
Get work done—meetings			✗				
Get work done—calls			✗				
Connect—Spend time with friends		✗		✓		✓	✓
Connect—Meet new people		✗		✗			
Connect—Feel close to family	✗						
Connect—Feel part of the community				✗			
Be entertained—music		✗					
Be entertained—games				✓			
Maintain wellbeing—Have daily ritual					✓		
Maintain wellbeing—Take a break							✓

"Now what patterns do you see?" Alex asked.

Jordan studied the map for a moment. "The first thing I see is that the job that seems to be best satisfied—and to matter to several different segments—is the one about connecting with friends."

"Yes," agreed Alex. "That's a key insight—and a helpful pattern these maps often reveal. It's a pretty good assumption that the core of Tazza's most loyal customers are people trying to get that job done. This is consistent with what we learned from Cate."

Alex circled the pattern on the map to make that point.

Market map for: **Circumstances**

Tazza

Jobs		Amelia—Late morning	Amelia—Saturday night	Mike—Mobile worker	The 3 Friends—Retired	Maggie—Early morning	Maggie—After workout	Olivia—After workout		
	Get work done—computer	✓		X						
	Get work done—meetings			X						
	Get work done—calls			X						
	Connect—Spend time with friends		X		✓		✓	✓		
	Connect—Meet new people		X		X					
	Connect—Feel close to	X								

"What else?"

"It looks like both Mike and Saturday night Amelia find Tazza to be a terrible solution for their jobs. I suppose that's another type of pattern—what segments we are serving where we are not doing very well."

This time, Jordan circled the patterns.

"Agreed. Anything else?" Alex asked.

"I guess it strikes me that the places Tazza plays today—where all the check marks and Xs are—are all over the map," answered Jordan. "That means there's a pretty broad spectrum of customers hiring Tazza for different things."

"I noticed that too," said Alex. "That's another common pattern. It's sometimes a sign of a company spreading itself too thin—trying to appeal to too many different types of

Market map for: Circumstances

Tazza

Jobs	Amelia—Late morning	Amelia—Saturday night	Mike—Mobile worker	The 3 Friends—Retired	Maggie—Early morning	Maggie—After workout	Olivia—After workout
Get work done—computer	✓		X				
Get work done—meetings			X				
Get work done—calls			X				
Connect—Spend time with friends		X		✓		✓	✓
Connect—Meet new people		X		X			
Connect—Feel close to family	X						
Connect—Feel part of the community				X			
Be entertained—music		X					
Be entertained—games				✓			
Maintain wellbeing					✓		

customers and ending up with a one-size-fits-none solution. That often goes along with losing focus on what really matters to your best customers—which can result in the type of decline we're seeing with Tazza.

"Lastly, we should note all of the blank boxes. These are places that Tazza does *not* play today—at least based on the handful of interviews we've done. When we're thinking about ways Tazza might grow, those could be options to consider. But that's for another day."

Jordan appreciated the visual depiction of what they'd learned so far and was struck by how straightforward it was to create. "It's so simple, but it already gives us a good sense of what's going on. I guess our aim now is to make it better through more interviews?"

"Yes—more customer interviews, for starters, to validate and refine this initial map. We'll likely discover some more regions to add to it. We'll also want to speak to people who have fired Tazza, and of course investigate the competition for the places on the map where Tazza is playing. And by that I mean the real competition—not just other coffee shops."

Alex hesitated, then added as he started packing up his bag, "I suppose that last step is where things might get the most . . . how should I say this? *Exciting*. But what's the point of being a market detective if there isn't a little intrigue? You'll have some good stories to tell Mark. Anyway, we should get going—no time to waste."

"Um, Alex . . . what do you mean by 'intrigue'?" asked Jordan.

But Alex was already out the door and did not hear her question. Or, Jordan suspected, pretended not to.

12

THE BARISTA

The next few days followed a pattern of their own. Each morning Alex and Jordan would settle in a different Tazza location and interview customers until closing time. After each conversation they'd discuss any new insights and use them to refine their evolving market map. They'd alternate playing the lead role, and Jordan was pleased that by the end of the second day it seemed like second nature.

With a few exceptions, they discovered their initial market map had been surprisingly accurate. The main additions were people in what they labeled "on the go" circumstances at different times of the day. These were customers who would pop into a cafe to purchase a drink, snack, or meal, and either leave immediately or stay just long enough to consume it. The jobs they all hired Tazza for related to energy levels or states of mind, and included jobs Jordan captured as "fuel up," "stay alert," "recharge," or "get an energy boost."

But for people who stayed longer in the cafes, Jordan and Alex found their initial map captured their jobs well.

Alex emphasized that this was not uncommon. "People often assume you have to talk to far more people than you really do to get the level of insights you need. In practice if you have two to three conversations for each area of the map, that's usually enough."

Their last destination was Tazza's highest-performing cafe, located in the neighboring state of Rhode Island near the downtown area of its capital city, Providence. It had been the third to open and was now one of its most successful, even managing to defy the recent negative sales trends.

As usual, Jordan's photographic memory for the company's financials proved helpful. "This place was not doing so well until about three months ago," explained Jordan. "Its numbers had plateaued, but then it started to grow again. Slower than before, but still positive. Not sure why. Rob thinks it's related to the corporate partnership program he launched around that time. It's run out of this location by a guy named James Finley. He's also the head barista. We have time with him first thing this morning to discuss."

Having completed enough outside interviews to form unbiased impressions, Alex was now more open to speaking with Tazza employees. James would be the first, at Cate's suggestion, as she believed he understood Tazza's current and former customers as well as anyone.

They found James behind the coffee bar teaching a novice barista the finer points of latte art. Two fresh lattes were set on the counter, one with an elegant leaf pattern formed in the thin foam layer that served as a canvas. The second was the focus of the trainee, who was attempting to copy this pattern under James's close supervision.

James looked up as they approached. "You must be Alex and Jordan!" he said. "So nice to meet you. Cate has raved about you both. And don't let her pleasant demeanor fool you, she's a very tough person to impress. How can I help?"

James was tall and lanky with a close-cropped splotch of black hair and several days of free-range beard growth. He looked to be in his mid-thirties, and wore the standard Tazza uniform of black jeans, sneakers, and a black T-shirt, this time inscribed with a quote from T. S. Eliot: "I have measured out my life with coffee spoons." He radiated a cheerful, upbeat energy, and seemed to have a permanently empathetic expression that Alex imagined must endear him to customers of all ages.

"Cate speaks highly of you too," said Alex. "Thanks for meeting us. We have a bunch of questions, but before we start grilling you, we'd love to hear about your background and role at Tazza today."

"Sure thing," James responded. "I've been around almost since the beginning. Joined part-time as a barista while I was in school. Such a fun job. I'm a pretty social guy, love meeting new people, so it was a great fit. Already had a passion for coffee too, so enjoyed learning more about that. That's when I mastered the craft of latte art." He gestured toward the trainee. "Franklin here just started learning today—but you can tell he's going to be a master. Look at the curvature and integrity of those fronds. Nice."

Franklin reacted to this praise with a faint smile but remained intensely focused on his fronds.

"When I graduated Cate asked me to come on board full-
time. I think she was impressed by my work ethic. Since I
wanted to get real-world work experience, I said yes. Tazza
was pretty small, so I got the chance to do all kinds of things.
Back in those days we didn't really worry about titles, everyone just jumped in and did whatever was needed. I've always
been kind of a jack-of-all-trades here, but I most enjoyed
any opportunity to interact with customers. Ended up managing the barista team, and developed and led their training
program—Barista Onboarding at Tazza. The BOAT program. Kind of corny, I know—but lends itself to all kinds of
dumb jokes . . . we're all in the same boat . . . let's row in the
same direction . . . What's a training program without corny
jokes? The baristas are so important—they're who the customers see first, you know? And what they remember. Cate
thought so too, so she created the head barista position. That
was my job until about three months ago.

"Speaking of which, here comes one of our newest grad-
uates with drinks for a special guest."

A young woman approached with a tray carrying two
lattes destined for a nearby table. She held them out for display, apparently looking for a sign of approval from James.
One had the familiar fern-leaf pattern, the other the number
thirty-seven on it.

"These look terrific," he said. He turned to Alex and Jordan, proud of his student. "Here you see two different latte

art techniques. The leaf is made by free pouring—you create it while the milk is poured into the espresso. The number is made by etching—basically you draw it using a coffee stirrer. See that couple over there? The woman is Amara. Today is her thirty-seventh birthday, so Anna added that little custom touch for her. That's her husband, Owen, with her. He doesn't even notice the art, so he just gets the standard leaf. Well done, Anna!"

Anna smiled wordlessly and carted them away to the nearby table. James watched her deliver them, then waved to Amara and shouted, "Happy birthday!" This prompted the entire cafe to break into the celebratory song while Amara beamed and Owen looked slightly embarrassed. Jordan noticed everyone seemed to know her name when they reached the "Happy birthday, dear Amara" line.

James turned back and said, "Sorry about that. Tazza tradition. The new baristas here still check some things with me, even though I had to put the training program on hold. Too busy to oversee it everywhere else like I used to."

"Lovely tradition," replied Alex. "You mentioned you came here about three months ago. What prompted the move?"

"Oh yeah. I came here to launch SIP—that's our corporate partnership program. SIP stands for Strategic Influencer Partnerships. Pretty good name, eh? I thought of it. But the program was Rob's idea. When he came in he brought a bunch of ideas for growing our customer base—mostly by pulling in new people from other places, like bars, corporate cafes, shared workspaces, even convenience stores. Idea behind the SIP program is to sell memberships to companies that give their employees discounts in our cafes. We get revenue from the companies and from the additional traffic it drives.

"I started working out of the Providence location to run the program—we decided to run SIP from here since we had extra office space and it's easier to get to all our other cafes. Don't have to fight traffic in and out of Boston. We did the pilot here and now I spend a lot of time visiting local companies near each cafe and pitching the program to them."

"How's the program going?" asked Jordan.

"Too early to tell, I guess," James continued. "It must be doing some good because this cafe we're in now has really seen an uptick since we started the pilot. And it makes sense, don't you think? Plus, none of us really have corporate experience like Rob, so if it works for a big company like he was at, it must be good enough for a small one like ours. I think he's planning to do some focus groups next week with our initial partners to get some feedback."

"Well, in any case it's very impressive, all that you've accomplished," Alex said. "How are you feeling about the IPO?"

James looked a little nervous. "Mixed feelings, really. On the one hand it's great for people working here—and for me personally. Will pay for my MBA—I've always planned to go back to school at some point. On the other hand, part of what makes Tazza special is the kind of magical feeling it gives people. I'm a little worried that once we are a public company that will change."

"Let's talk about that magical feeling," said Alex. "Even with the recent challenges, Tazza customers have a reputation of being fanatical about the place. Why do you think that is?"

James reflected for a moment. "*Fanatical* is a good word for it. It reminds me of the way people feel about their favorite sports teams. Tazza customers are kind of like that. I don't mean they are cheering for us to beat our competitors . . . although one time a guy came in claiming he'd reverse engineered the recipes for all of Stella's signature drinks . . . Don't worry: we ignored it! But Tazza has always been a place where people connect—just like going to games and rooting for a team connects you to a community with a shared purpose. The other thing following a local team does is make you feel like a local—even if you're not from around here. Hanging out at Tazza creates this same feeling, and intentionally so: the design of each cafe reflects the feel of the local neighborhood, and there are lots of longtime residents in each cafe community."

"Until recently," he added with a sigh.

Before he could go further, they were again interrupted, this time by a middle-aged woman who was clearly an actual sports fan, as she was attired in sweatpants, a sweatshirt, and a cap all embroidered with the same local team logo.

"James! What are you doing here?" the woman asked.

"Nicole! What are *you* doing here is a better question? So great to see you!"

As she moved in to give James a bear hug, he explained, "Nicole is one of those longtime Tazza fanatics—used to see her all the time at my old location."

"Just visiting my mother," she said. "She lives south of here at an assisted living facility. As you know, I'm addicted to Tazza's Hazelnut Eyeopener blend, so decided to drop in on my way down. I can't tell you how much we miss you back in Boston! Place is not the same without you."

She turned to Alex and Jordan and said, "James is the world's greatest barista. Literally. Well, almost literally. Did you know he came in fourth at the World Barista Championship in Madrid?"

Alex and Jordan did not.

"Now he's a big-shot executive," she continued. "But he always used to listen to me complain about my dating life, sometimes for hours. Even introduced me to my current boyfriend. *And* found someone to rent a room in my house when I was looking for a subletter. He was better than a therapist."

"A lot cheaper too," joked James.

"Maybe I scared you away?"

"Never!" James assured her. "You're always welcome to come by here—would love to catch up. Excuse me just one moment—need to check on the morning's deliveries. Be right back."

James exited to the kitchen while Nicole continued to rave about him.

"James was so important to me when I first moved to the area. Took the time to get to know me and always made me feel special. Not a lot of people do that when you move to a new place, especially when you're older. People already have families or are just set in their routines. Anyway, I have to run or I'll miss mom's bingo hour. She's only five feet tall and ninety-two years old, but does she get fierce when she plays bingo! I gotta be there to rein her in—she sits next to her best friend, Martha, and I swear mom would body slam her if I wasn't there. Please give James my best! And lovely to meet you."

Alex and Jordan exchanged smiles as they both took a breath. Before either could comment on the morning's whirlwind of activity, James was back.

"So . . . where were we?" he asked. "Anything else I can help you with?"

"There is one other thing," said Alex. "We'd like to talk to some people who used to be loyal customers at Tazza but have left. We have one name so far—Barb Asheville—but were hoping you could connect us with a few others."

"I know Barb! Tell her I said hello. Yeah, I can send you some names. Many people I know who left still keep in touch with me. Oh—and you should definitely talk to the Mayor. If you can find him, that is."

"Who's the Mayor?" asked Alex.

"I'm surprised you don't know about him," answered James. "He's probably the best customer in the history of Tazza. Kind of a celebrity too—internally anyway. Just loved the place. Was a real shock when he stopped showing up. I think it was his disappearance that finally pushed Cate to hire you. He must have spent a small fortune on Tazza over the years."

"Wait—is that Ed Amato?" Jordan asked.

"Yeah. You know him?"

Jordan explained her recent analysis of the Connoisseurs' Club and how its members were chosen. She remembered Ed's name because he was number one on the list her algorithm generated.

"Certainly sounds like a great person to talk to," Alex observed. "Anything you can tell us about him?"

"Friendliest guy you're ever likely to meet. Older, probably late sixties. Came over when he was a kid from Italy with his father. Will talk to anyone about anything—and if he starts a conversation, I guarantee he won't be the one to end it. Just loves people. We called him the Mayor of Tazza because he was always around and you felt like he was looking out for everyone who came in. Also an absolute soccer nut. Watches every game he can on TV and obsesses about player statistics. I think he played at one point when he was younger, somewhere in Italy. Not professional, but even amateurs over there are crazy talented. I think it's genetic. Or maybe it's the pasta?"

"Not sure about that," replied Alex. "But it would be great if we could find him. Former customers who used to be so loyal are always a source of great insight. Any idea where he is?"

For the first time, James looked a bit downcast. "None. I know he was having some health problems just before he disappeared. Said his doctor told him he needed to stop sitting around in cafes so much and get out and get some

exercise. He's been spotted a couple of times by other customers, but no one knows where he's spending all his time
now. You know what? You could ask Barb if she knows
anything—they used to talk for hours whenever Barb made
it to Boston."

Alex thanked him, and he and Jordan relocated to a nearby
table to prepare for their last day of customer interviews.

"Fascinating," Alex said, and then noticed Jordan's pen-
sive demeanor. "Any observations?"

"Not sure," she replied. "It sounds like the SIP program
has been pretty successful . . . but there's something about
it that doesn't quite make sense. Can't put my finger on it."

"Perhaps it will come to you later," Alex said. "For now,
let's shift into the beginner's mindset one last time and gather
a bit more small data on current customers. Tomorrow we'll
follow a different path—people who fired Tazza."

13

RISING STAKES

R ob. Call me."
   Cate's text popped up on the dashboard of Rob's web-connected BMW during his evening commute home. Its urgency made him sufficiently nervous that he pulled over at the next highway rest stop to call her back.

"Got your message—what's up, Cate?"

"Quick update on the offsite: just heard that in addition to two of our board members, the senior banker handling our IPO has asked to join. I'm letting everyone know so we can prepare accordingly."

Rob tried to sound unconcerned, but there was a slight strain in his voice as he responded.

"That can only be a good thing, right Cate? Once he sees everything we're doing to turn things around the IPO should cruise ahead."

"That's the goal. You have a starring role in achieving it. What are you planning to present?"

Rob reviewed his three-part plan to drive growth: the CCC program to sell more to existing customers, the partnership initiative focused on corporate sales and driving traffic from their employees, and the menu expansion program to siphon off customers from other segments, including bars, restaurants, and convenience stores.

"That sounds good," said Cate. "Given the IPO is happening soon we'll need to make some hard decisions on which paths to pursue. Just not enough time or resources to do everything. So anything you can share on initial results or ROI for these will help us prioritize."

Rob was wary of this line of inquiry. "Sure, Cate. Of course these things take time to show results. I mean we're really looking to move to another level of scale, so we have to launch advanced programs that work in larger organizations. But I should have some directional numbers for the group."

Although he knew he couldn't commit to impressive numbers, he was optimistic this would be an opportunity for him to shine in front of the board. The thought gave him enough confidence to ask a question.

"So I heard that consultant is going to be there. Do you think that's necessary at this stage?"

The line was silent for a moment. Then Cate said, "I do. He has some interesting new ways to look at our customers and where we are today, and it can't hurt to have a different point of view. Plus, Jordan's been helping him out, and it will be nice to have her work recognized."

Jordan's unexpected transfer out of Rob's orbit, though temporary, was a sore spot for him. But he knew better than to mention this.

"Great! I'm sure you're right, Cate. I look forward to hearing what he has to say."

After they hung up, Rob worried he'd gone too far by questioning Alex's participation. Of course Cate would insist on this! Otherwise she'd look foolish for paying Alex all that money.

But his concerns dissipated as he thought more about the possibilities of the offsite. There was no way he wouldn't be the star of the show. Pretty much everything they had underway was Rob's idea. Who else there could possibly offer any useful ideas?

14

FIRED

Alex reached Barb using the email address Gerald had given him. She agreed to meet them at the Greenwich Club, a nearby country club known for its immaculate, championship-level golf course and lofty membership fees.

"Any friend of Gerald's is a friend of mine!" read her email. "Meet you in the lobby at 10:00 right after Jill and I finish terrifying the local bird population with our wild tennis shots. Jill swears we beaned a pigeon yesterday but nobody was ever recovered. That's my story and I'm sticking to it ha ha!"

Alex picked up Jordan and they headed over together, arriving fifteen minutes ahead of time. The spacious lobby of the Greenwich Club was lined on both sides with high oak bookshelves, each stocked with long rows of dark bound tomes, framed ancient maps, and a collection of old globes inscribed with borders centuries out of date. To Jordan, the vibe was more monastic library than stuffy watering hole.

Just after a distant clock chimed ten, two elegantly per-spiring, silver-ponytailed women in white tennis skirts and matching polos bounded into the lobby through the rear doors leading to the club beyond. They were slightly out of breath as they strode up to Alex and Jordan.

"Well hello, young man! And young *lady*, of course. I'm Barb. Pleased to make your acquaintance. This is Jill. Why don't y'all come on back to the terrace? We'll have a drink and become besties!"

Jill placed her hand on Alex's arm and whispered, "The Bloody Marys at Chesterfield's are to die for. You simply *must* try one." She moved closer and added, "*Or three.*"

Alex gave what he hoped was a noncommittal nod, ex-changed amused looks with Jordan, and followed the women as they relocated to the terrace restaurant. The hostess led them to an outdoor table with a prime view of the first two holes of the golf course ("The front of the front nine!" Barb quipped) spread out before them and meandering into a multihued horizon of pine trees and carefully coiffed greens.

Before Alex could protest, Jill ordered a round of drinks for everyone and Barb kicked things off.

"So! How is Gerald doing? And those two pals of his? Still stinging from all the cash they lost to me at poker?"

Alex chuckled. "They seemed to be doing well. We only spoke for a short time. Didn't get into the history of who won what—but I gathered your games were quite competitive."

"Absolutely," affirmed Barb. "Ya gotta keep score, right? Jill here is a worthy opponent. We battle it out pretty much every morning, like two titans. Or titanesses? Is that a word, dear?"

This question seemed to be directed at Jordan, so she responded with an uncertain shrug.

"Then we cool down with Chesterfield's special recipe," added Jill. "They *fortify* their Bloody Marys with karela juice. Secret ingredient. Makes the calories just melt off."

This claim seemed dubious, but no one debated it.

"So, what can we do for y'all?" Barb asked.

"We're working for Tazza," Alex said, "researching how to do a better job for our customers. That's what brought us to Gerald and his friends. He mentioned you used to be a regular there, so we thought it made sense to speak with you too."

"I see. Well, I'll tell you I'm not really a customer anymore. Used to be. I had a blast with those guys, used to meet for games several times a week. But not so much anymore."

"That's one reason we were eager to talk to you—to understand why you left," said Alex. "Before we get there, perhaps we could go back to the beginning of your relationship with Tazza—if I could call it that. When did you first start going?"

"Oh my . . . that *was* a long time ago. What was it, Jill? Maybe eight years ago? Must have been. It was right after I moved into an apartment. My daughter finally talked me into selling our old family house. I'd been rattling around by myself for years. Just got to be too much with the maintenance and all . . . things always breaking. And not as much fun in an empty nest. So I moved into town—closer to my kids. Two of 'em work and live nearby. Bobby's a teacher and Zoe's a doctor. I think it gives them peace of mind to have me where they can keep an eye on me. Funny how you start out taking care of your kids and they end up taking care of you, eh?"

Alex could relate to this. Even though he was at the age when both his parents and kids were largely self-sufficient, he knew that he might be nearing a tipping point of sorts.

"What made you first try out Tazza? And why did you keep going?"

By now Jordan was familiar enough with Alex's method that she recognized Alex cycling through the first few job spec questions. He'd explained the method was similar even if you were speaking to people who had fired your products—you were still looking for the same information defined by the job spec.

"Well, I couldn't help but stumble onto it, it's right in my neighborhood. I'm a coffee lover, so I don't need to be pushed to try out a new place. I guess you could say Tazza and I just clicked. People there were so welcoming and friendly. The staff too. Made new friends right away, and it became like a second home."

"Why do you think a 'second home' was important at that time in your life?"

"Oh, I don't know . . . I suppose because I was in kind of a funk from moving out of my house. Thirty years of memories . . . all my kids grew up there. And all those dreams when Barry and I first moved in. Barry was my husband—he passed ten years ago. I felt kind of lost when I moved, like my whole frame of reference for life had suddenly evaporated. Felt that way when Barry died too. The cafe crew made me feel like I mattered again, like I had a group of people I fit into. Maybe it helped me create a new sense of identity? Or got me started anyway, after I kind of lost my old one. That's probably it. Of course I had my kids nearby, but they are so busy with their lives and kids of their own."

"Thank you for sharing that with us, Barb," Alex said. "I can understand how you would feel that way. It's wonderful you found that new community when you needed one."

This exchange had sobered the mood a bit, so Alex shifted gears.

"You said that you no longer frequent the cafe. What changed?"

"Hmm . . . I'd felt for a while that things were changing. Slowly at first, then more suddenly. What makes a place feel like home anyway? Familiar faces, familiar surroundings. Has to have some kind of stability. Having new people to meet is nice too, but felt like the whole crowd changed too fast. Not just the faces, but different type of people—not as interested in talking to each other. More people jabbering on their phones, staring at their screens . . . and those business people—sheesh! So antisocial, like they were too busy running the world.

"Then they kept changing the space itself—smaller tables, I guess so more people could work, and they were making room for that big conference room no one uses. Waste of space if you ask me. Lots of new food, new drinks, even started selling trinkets and what not. Started to feel just like any other coffee chain. Then once some of my friends started leaving . . . well, that was it for me."

Barb paused to rest, as if recounting her breakup with Tazza was wearing her out.

"This is really helpful, Barb," said Alex. "So now you come to this club—would you say this place for you is the new Tazza?"

"Absolutely. All the time I used to spend there I now spend here."

"Why do you prefer it?"

"Well, it's not perfect, but it's for the same reasons I used to love Tazza. See lots of the same faces when I come here, and there are things to do to keep you occupied. Tennis, or golf, or several bridge clubs that meet here. One thing that's even better than Tazza: they host events for meeting new people. People of a certain age, if you know what I mean. Also, you pay for a membership here—so you feel like you can hang out however long you want, come and go as you please. Sometimes at Tazza I felt a little guilty for being there all the time, because I knew I was taking a spot another customer could be in. Plus, I can get some exercise here, you know? Have to keep my girlish figure!"

"That makes sense, Barb," said Alex. "Your comment about sports reminds me of one other question I have for you: Do you know Ed Amato?"

"The Mayor—of course! All the regulars knew him, even those like me who didn't go to his home base cafe in Boston very often. We joked he must sleep in the storage room on a stack of coffee beans every night, he was there so often. Wonderful man!"

"Any idea why he left, or where he is now? We'd love to talk to him too."

"Not sure—maybe for the same reasons as me? Don't know where he is though—it's weird, because I still keep in touch with all my other old Tazza friends, though not as much as I'd like. But no one's seen him lately. There is one person who might know. Hey, Coach! Can you come over here for a sec?"

Coach, it turned out, was also known as Liam and the tennis instructor at the Greenwich Club. He grinned as he sauntered to their table in response to Barb's summons.

"Hey, young ladies! Great game today. What can I do for you?" he asked.

"Didn't you say you met Ed Amato at that soccer event you went to last week?"

"Yes! He came to our New England Ultras outing—that's our soccer supporters' group. I remember him because he was a new face. Really nice guy—talked everyone's ears off!"

"That sounds like Ed," Barb said.

"What's a soccer supporters' group?" asked Jordan.

"The craziest, most devoted fans of a local professional team. We rally people at the games, hold up those giant banners (heavier than they look!), lead cheers and songs, sometimes transport people there and back. Make sure everyone has plenty of team swag. Oh, and in our case we host amateur soccer games at the stadium on weekends. I'm the coach of that team too. It's great fun. Ed came to our game last week—he was actually pretty good—must be his Italian genes! Not sure if he'll be back, we'll see. Hope so."

Liam glanced at his watch. "Hey, I gotta run—have another coaching session starting now. Oh, Barb—I left the number of that physical therapist for your daughter at the front desk. Hope he helps. See you Wednesday, ladies!"

As Liam departed, Barb picked up where she left off. "Love that man. Always takes the time to listen to my problems and help out. More than just a tennis coach—coaches me on life too! Right, Jill?"

"Liam's a gem," Jill agreed. "You know, Barb, we should probably get going too."

"Yes, sorry folks—Jill and I are heading to the spa now. Please give us a jingle if you want to chat again. Good luck with your stuff!"

Alex thanked them, and he and Jordan packed up and walked out to the parking lot. At the car Jordan asked what Alex thought of this new information about Ed.

"It's interesting, but feels like a dead end to me," Alex said. "It's clear Ed loves soccer, but it's hard to imagine the supporters' club experience could compete with Tazza for the jobs that were most important to him. Have you seen those people at the games? They are so loud, it's impossible to hear the person next to you, and we know Ed loves conversation more than anything. A lot of rowdy younger people too—often intoxicated. Again, doesn't fit with what we know about him. Maybe we'll get some new clues on his whereabouts when we start investigating the Tazza competitors tomorrow."

"Yeah, you're probably right," Jordan said. But as they drove away, she couldn't shake the feeling they were missing something. Normally she liked crossing off potential solutions to a problem; it narrowed the options and simplified the process. But in this case, it just made things seem more mysterious than ever.

15

THE REAL COMPETITION

The next phase of their investigation was the most logistically complex, as Alex and Jordan planned to visit the wide range of Tazza competitors identified in the interviews. The list was formed by reviewing what customers had shared about other solutions they hired to get specific jobs done, and then adding any companies Tazza was explicitly targeting with its growth strategy. They settled on four types of competitors: food chains, shared workspaces, bars, and the eight-hundred-pound gorilla of the coffee industry, Stella's.

"This will be a long day," Alex observed. "We'll have to be very focused since we only have until tomorrow to investigate competitors. And we need to leave time to develop our conclusions for the executive team. The good news is we'll follow exactly the same method we've been using: talk to customers in these places and use the job spec questions as our guide. We're looking for all the same information—circumstances, jobs, what they hire today, help wanted signs, and so on. It's just a different set of customers. What's first up on our list?"

Jordan consulted her planner. "We said we'd start with a healthy fast-food competitor chain—the one I suggested is called Santé. They have restaurants in all our neighborhoods, often on the same block as us. Sometimes even two or three locations within a few blocks. Very generic, but it's been growing like crazy. Getting even a little share of their business would be tremendous."

"Possibly," replied Alex. "It depends on at what cost."

"How so?"

"You might gain share, but it could dilute the appeal to your best, most loyal customers. Not always, but just a risk to consider. Plus, you might have to work very hard to get it. But this is exactly the type of thing we'll explore today."

As they entered the first restaurant, Jordan tapped Alex on the shoulder and whispered dramatically, *"The game is afoot."*

Alex gave her a good-natured eye roll.

"Sorry couldn't resist . . . I've been saving that and waiting for the right opportunity to say it all morning."

Santé was part of the emerging fast-casual dining trend, distinguishing itself from traditional fast-food chains by featuring healthier food options prepared from fresh ingredients each day. The menu was largely stable, with meals, snacks, and drinks for any time of day stocked in self-serve displays near quick-moving payment lines. Its modern decor included a mix of burgundy colors, leather benches, and wooden tables, giving it a vaguely Parisian feel and an air of sophistication that belied its international chain identity.

"These things are everywhere now," observed Jordan. "And they do a great business—just look at the lines up-front, and how fast they are moving. Rob saw this as an opportunity—it's the motivation behind his menu expansion initiative—get more of these on-the-go eaters."

They grabbed snacks from the kiosk, paid, filled cups from a self-serve coffee station, and sat at one of the few small tables arrayed against the walls. It was immediately clear the place wasn't designed for people to linger or have extended conversations. The tables were just too small and there were too few of them on the limited floor space. They observed most people just purchasing their food and leaving; those who did sit at a table remained only long enough to eat.

The rapid turnover of diners made it easy to pack multiple conversations into a short period of time. These interviews confirmed their initial impressions: people hired Santé for the job of eating a relatively healthy meal while on the go. Most worked nearby and carried food away to eat back at their office, at a nearby park, or in some other outdoor space. They hired Santé because the food was healthy, fresh, affordable, and above all quick. They also liked the predictability of what they were getting, and many had favorite food items they'd eat multiple times per week.

The ability to complete several interviews in a short time also proved beneficial when they were approached by a concerned Santé employee.

"Excuse me, can I ask what you are doing here?" she asked.

"Two reasons," answered Alex. "We're enjoying these delicious Santé Sunrise Breakfast Salads—love the idea of a breakfast salad—very innovative—and fueling up with two large coffees for a busy day of work. Also, we're talking to some of the customers here to understand why people choose Santé as their preferred dining option."

The employee gave them a stern look. "I'm glad you're enjoying your meals, and we appreciate your business. However, our policy is that we don't allow people to bother our customers for commercial reasons. I'm going to have to ask you both to leave."

Alex seemed unfazed by this, which reduced Jordan's alarm, as she couldn't remember the last time she'd been in any kind of trouble. Nevertheless, she was moved to protest.

"We're not bothering them. We're just trying to understand the jobs they are trying to get done—and why they hire Santé. We only talk to people who are receptive—just ask Clarence here, he was happy to talk to us."

"It's OK, Jordan," Alex said. "Santé has a right to provide or refuse service to anyone it likes." Turning to the Santé employee, he said, "We understand and respect your policy. We'll be on our way."

As they exited to the street, Alex said, "Congratulations—you've just been kicked out of your first competitor stakeout."

"So this is what you meant by 'intrigue.' I guess this is normal?"

"It's not uncommon. But there is nothing unethical, illegal, or underhanded about what we are doing. Quite the contrary. We are engaged in a noble mission: understanding what customers really want so we can create things that improve their lives. That's the beauty of these small data activities. Everything is up-front, and it's mostly through direct conversations with people that they are happy to engage in. We're not trying to uncover secrets about people they don't want us to know—but the ones they do. It's even possible our conclusions will benefit Santé. Although I understand why they may not see it that way."

Santé restaurants really were everywhere, so they quickly visited two more, confirming but adding nuance to their initial findings. Santé was focused squarely on solving the nourishment needs of the on-the-go eater, and they optimized the experience with healthy, affordable food choices; high-quality, fresh ingredients; rapid service; and a largely stable menu with only slight novelty each day. The coffee was nothing to get excited about, but good enough to purchase along with lunch or breakfast.

Also consistent was getting ejected from these two other locations. This became a source of pride for Jordan, though she wondered if there was now a back room somewhere with their pictures on a wall under the header "Santé's Most Wanted." Fortunately, they wrapped up their fast-casual competitor investigation and moved on before they could find out.

"OK, one competitor type down, three left: bars, shared workspaces, and of course Stella's," said Jordan. "Which should we do next?"

"Let's start with workspaces," replied Alex. "That way we'll cover bars toward the end of the day when they're likely to be busier."

"Cool. These are the places Mike the business guy detested, right? Didn't he complain about pets there or something?"

"That's right. Mike didn't like puppies. Think about that for a moment. In my view, puppies could only improve any office environment."

"The more puppies the better," Jordan agreed.

Office Oasis, like Santé, was another trend-riding phenom, in this case the explosion of coworking facilities aimed at nomadic professionals, independent contractors, or any organization looking to reduce overhead costs and increase flexibility. Some offered nothing but a place to sit for the day with the barest of support infrastructure. Others provided services such as printing, videoconferencing, and even in-house legal advice. The most advanced went even further by aspiring to create a sense of community among its members. Office Oasis was in this last category.

Jordan secured a room for them to use for the afternoon, but after dropping off their belongings they immediately headed to the common area to start their investigation. A number of tables were scattered around the open space, and an island at the center was stocked with an array of snacks and beverages. Off to one side was a large conference room with a transparent glass wall, through which they could see a high-powered-looking executive team engaged in what appeared to be an intense negotiation.

They approached the island's coffee station, where two professionals wearing the universal uniform of the management-consultant foot soldier—blue blazer, white shirt, slate-gray dress pants—were chatting.

"Excuse me," said Alex, mentally shifting to language he thought would connect with them. "We're doing some research on the value proposition of this place, and were hoping to ask you a few questions—will just take a few minutes."

Both men looked less than excited about this, but agreed without questioning Alex's motives. *Perhaps they assume this will be over faster if they don't waste time asking us what we are up to,* thought Jordan.

"What brings you here today?" Alex asked.

The older of the two answered first. "In town for a client meeting. We work for a midsize consulting firm, so we don't have offices in many cities. Our firm is a member of this place so we can bring clients here for larger meetings if we need to. And have a place to work while we're in town."

"Makes sense. How do you like it here?"

"It's OK. Beats working in a hotel room or a cafe like Stella's or something like that. At least it has a semblance of a professional environment, so it's OK to meet clients here. Still not as good as if we had our own offices in this city, but we can't afford them. I used to work for one of the big firms, and they have premium locations with high-end office environments—spared no expense. When clients came to see you there, they were impressed."

"Why is it important that they be impressed by your office spaces?" asked Jordan.

"In our business, it's a sign of credibility. Signals we are a premium firm and justifies the premium fees we charge. Plus, clients assume that if a firm can afford to have a high-end office space, they must be successful. Gives them confidence they are hiring a high-quality outfit."

His younger colleague spoke up, adding, "That's all academic of course. We're here because we don't have that option."

"You mentioned your other options are things like hotels or cafes," said Alex. "I think I know the answer to this question, but what's wrong with those places?"

"Cafes are the opposite extreme of the high-end office space. Just not professional—can't have client meetings there. And very noisy, so hard to do calls or even concentrate on work. Office Oasis is quieter. Some of the conference rooms are pretty nice if you're willing to pay, so clients feel comfortable in them. Plus, they have stuff like high-quality printers or videoconference rooms if we need them. Ever try printing something in a hotel business center? Their computers and printers are usually ten years old and always breaking. Time is always scarce—we need predictability. Don't want any surprises. At least here we know what we'll get, regardless of the city we're in."

"Anything you don't like about it?"

"Well, it's still obvious that we're just squatting here, but nothing to be done about that. And some of the people here are not exactly on-brand for us." He gestured toward two young men seated nearby dressed in jeans, sneakers, and baseball caps. "Also hard to predict or control everything the client experiences—you never know who will be walking through or what they'll be doing."

"Actually, I like that about this place," said his junior colleague. "Maybe it's a generational thing. I feel like these are my people. I like that they make an effort to encourage a sense of community here. You can build your business network, but also socialize a bit."

Jordan wondered if the young man was concerned he'd expressed a nonconformist view, because he added, "One thing we can both agree on: the coffee here is terrible. We've complained, but I don't think it's important to them. I can understand, it's not part of their business model. Anyway, we should probably get to work—nice chatting with you."

Alex and Jordan stayed in the common area for two hours and managed to speak to a dozen other patrons. The primary circumstances they discovered were people in town for meetings, independent contractors or freelancers who had no other office space, and people who lived in town but worked remotely for larger companies. Most of the jobs they hired Office Oasis for were functional, but many people emphasized the social and emotional benefits. These were most apparent in the views shared by a young freelancer.

"I love working for myself," he said. "I'm a coder. My business is really successful—I even make more money than most of my friends working for big companies. But sometimes I still feel insecure about it. Working for a company gives you a sense of professional identity—affects not just how you feel about yourself, but how your friends or family view you. I miss that sometimes. Coming here gives me a little of that feeling. It also gives me a sense of routine and forces me to get out of the house and put myself together. You've heard that word *adulting*? It means doing things that make you feel grown-up. I always thought it was pretty silly until I experienced the need for it myself.

"It can be lonely working for yourself, too, so I get to meet and talk to other people here. I guess it's another reason I like working in this place."

In late afternoon, when they felt like they were reaching the point of diminishing returns, they headed to the next type of competitor on their list, in this case represented by a bar called O'Sullivan's.

"This is the same place Gerald mentioned when we spoke to them," Jordan said. Although they'd avoided ejection from Office Oasis, she was naturally more concerned about their next destination.

"You know they have bouncers at bars, right, Alex?"

"Good point. But we'll be OK. Remember: when you're up-front about what you're doing, and your motives are pure, people will give you the benefit of the doubt. We might want to leave our notebooks in the car though. Help us blend in."

O'Sullivan's, in contrast to the chains they'd visited earlier, had only one small, cozy location on a street corner in downtown Boston. At five-thirty in the afternoon, it was already standing-room only as the after-work crowd took advantage of the abundant happy hour fare.

They nevertheless managed to secure a narrow span of bar real estate as two men received their drink order and vacated it in search of greener pastures. Oldies rock blared from overhead loudspeakers, which, combined with the voices shouting over it, made hearing one another nearly impossible. The crowd was on the young side, late twenties or early thirties on average, and a mix of what looked like local workers, young professionals, and students.

"How are we going to talk to anyone here?" shouted Jordan. "I'm yelling and I can't even hear my own voice!"

"Let's observe for a while and see what we learn that way," Alex shouted back. "Then we can see if it's easier to hear at one of those tables over there. If that fails maybe we step outside and talk to people."

Jordan mouthed OK and they both leaned against the counter. Looking around, she observed small clusters of mostly men or mostly women, many resigned to silence as their eyes constantly scanned the room for . . . what exactly? Other singles, perhaps. Or maybe looking for interesting distractions. Occasionally an outburst of laughter would break through the din, or enthusiastic reactions to the ceaseless shuttling of beverages from the bar.

What jobs were people trying to get done here? Jordan wondered. Meet the loves of their lives? Unwind after a long day? Make new friends? Find a mate? Descend into an abyss of nihilistic despair? She could imagine there were some jobs related to community here, but of a different variety than what was found at Tazza. Certainly people watching, entertainment. But real communication and connection? Seemed impossible.

Her thoughts were interrupted by the bartender asking what they'd like to drink. Alex ordered a beer, and though

Jordan didn't particularly want anything, she felt obligated to do likewise. *It's how you pay the rent for the bar space,* she thought, recalling the words of Amelia the college student.

After twenty minutes of unenthusiastic, shallow sips and people watching ("Definitely one job you can get done here!" Jordan yelled), the bar's steady state was perturbed by the arrival of a group of rowdy sports fans. They all wore attire with their team's logo—on hats, scarves, jerseys, sweatshirts—some even had it painted on their arms and faces. They appeared to be fueling up for the evening's game, and somehow, impossibly, managed to squeeze into the packed bar. Along with drinking, the group was engaged in a pregame ritual of songs and cheers, with themes of unbounded praise for their team and limitless scorn for their rivals. In contrast to everyone else, this group seemed to genuinely be having a great time.

Their leader came straight to the bar, where the bartender leaned over to give him a bear hug.

"Big Dog! What's the word?"

"My man! Warming up for the big game tonight," Big Dog said.

"Hook you up with the usual?" the bartender asked.

"For sure! Two pitchers tonight—got a big crowd."

"You got it," the bartender responded. He went to the tap and quickly produced two pitchers of the usual. Big Dog gave him a high five, then departed.

"Fascinating," Alex murmured to himself, then said to Jordan, "You know, maybe we should cut our losses here and head to Stella's. That's our last competitor type and we can debrief a bit. What do you think?"

"No argument here!"

Their encounter with Stella's was the least surprising of the day. A national chain with hundreds of cafes around the country, Stella's seemed defined most of all by uniformity. The interior looked exactly like every other Stella's Jordan had visited, with an expansive floorspace dotted with small tables and a handful of couches. Much of the space was devoted to displays of merchandise, giving it, to her, an unappealing commercial feel. She was struck by how few people seemed to be interacting: just a few groups limited to two, and many of these seemed to have the formality of work-related exchanges.

Feeling worn out from an intense day, they decided to defer more interviews and instead reflect on the day.

"What's surprising is I've always assumed the real competition for Tazza was mostly just other coffee places," Jordan said. "Like this place—or the big bookstore chains where they have cafes, or the little one-off spots. Even people staying at home and making their own coffee. But we spent the day at restaurants, office spaces, bars . . . completely different environments. And I'm not even sure we've hit all the competitors. I'm also struck by just *how many* different jobs people hire the same solution for. Like Office Oasis—everything from impressing demanding clients to feeling like a grown-up to meeting new people."

"Very true," agreed Alex. "When you look at the world through the jobs lens it can change not just *who* you see as competitors, but your understanding of *how* you compete with them. Often you find you're playing not just one but many competitive games at the same time, with different or even conflicting rules for how to win. It's why this map we are creating of the market landscape is so important, as it will orient us and help us see the big picture of everything that is going on. But we'll get to that tomorrow, on our last day."

16

CRACKING THE CASE

After another half day spent investigating the competition, some clear themes had emerged. The first was how narrowly focused each competitor appeared to be on solving for specific customer jobs. Santé, for example, aimed at satisfying the nourishment needs of the on-the-go eater. O'Sullivan's was optimized to help young people meet and connect with one another in a casual manner. Office Oasis, despite the misgivings of Mike, was quite well suited for the functional jobs of a large swath of mobile workers and freelancers.

This specialization was reinforced by the jobs they were *not* well suited for. Santé's limited floor space and small number of two-seat tables made it impossible to imagine lingering there to read, work, or socialize. O'Sullivan's clearly was not the place to take a restful break or engage in lengthy, in-depth conversations. Office Oasis made only a half-hearted attempt to solve for the jobs of people looking to connect, and even then focused on helping them to network professionally more than create personal relationships or a sense of community.

Using this information, Jordan created the final version of the Tazza market map. After expanding the set of latitude and longitude dimensions to capture the main jobs and circumstances they'd uncovered, she highlighted regions where each of the competitors seemed to focus.

Market map for:
Tazza

Circumstances

Jobs	Mike—Mobile worker	Amelia—Saturday night	Amelia—Late morning	The 3 Friends—Retired	Maggie—Early morning	Maggie—After workout	Olivia—After workout	On-the-go morning	On-the-go afternoon	On-the-go evening
Get work done—computer	X		✓							
Get work done—meetings	X									
Get work done—calls	X									
Connect—Meet new people	X	X		X						
Connect—Spend time with friends		X		✓		✓	✓			
Connect—Feel close to family										
Connect—Feel part of the community				✓						
Be entertained—live music		X								
Be entertained—games				✓						
Be entertained—watch sports				X						
Maintain wellbeing—Have daily ritual					✓					
Maintain wellbeing—Get an energy boost					✓			✓	✓	✓
Maintain wellbeing—Take a break							✓	✓		✓
Maintain wellbeing—Eat a snack								X	X	X
Maintain wellbeing—Eat a healthy meal								X	X	X

Office Oasis · O'Sullivan's · Santé

Back at Tazza headquarters, Jordan projected the map onto a wall-size screen and both she and Alex stepped back to study the overall picture.

"A fascinating result," Alex observed. "This map, combined with the details in the job specs we've created, should contain all the information we need to answer the central questions we set out to answer: Why does Tazza get hired, and why does it get fired? Jordan, you clearly have an uncanny talent for seeing useful patterns in data. Perhaps we should start with your observations?"

Jordan was happy to oblige, but studied the map for a full minute before speaking. "OK. On the question of why Tazza gets hired, I think there are two levels to my answer. The first level is simply the list of jobs we have here on the vertical axis of this map. Those were all discovered by talking to real customers, so it's reasonable to conclude that it's a pretty comprehensive list of jobs Tazza gets hired for today."

She continued her analysis while extracting a laser pointer from her backpack. "The second level is more nuanced, as you have to look at just the squares with check marks—those are the places Tazza gets hired *and* customers think it's a great solution for the job."

Aiming the pointer at the screen, she highlighted the job "connect—spend time with friends" with a small red dot. "Take this job here. Both Maggie and Olivia hire Tazza for it, and they are clearly happy with the results. They said it was because they can find a quiet table, they like the coffee, and it's close to where they meet for their workouts. It's not too crowded, so they feel like it's OK to hang out as long as they want. This example shows that to fully answer the question of why people hire Tazza, you have to identify their priority jobs *and* the reasons they think Tazza is a great solution."

"I agree with your conclusions," Alex said. "You've also listed several essential details of the Tazza experience that make it a good fit for those jobs. For other spots on the map—where the Xs are, as you've implied—Tazza is not as attractive."

"Does that mean Tazza shouldn't be trying to play there at all?" Jordan asked.

"Possibly—let's come back to that in a bit. First let's answer the other big question: Why is Tazza getting fired today?"

This was harder to answer, as they both concentrated intently on the screen for several minutes before Jordan finally spoke.

"For me, the first clues are where the competitors play. Those zones on the map overlap with places where Tazza gets hired but is not a good solution—thus all the Xs. Yet we also learned these competitors are *great solutions* for those same jobs and circumstances. That means those are just tough games for Tazza to win. It's possible that people try out Tazza for those jobs but then discover there are better solutions, so they fire it. That becomes even more likely as these chains grow and become more common in our neighborhoods."

Alex summed up, more for his own benefit than Jordan's. "So explanation number one is: competitors who are laser-focused on specific jobs are peeling off customers who weren't really that happy with Tazza's solution to begin with. Anything else?"

"Hmm . . . I'm thinking about Tazza's best customers," replied Jordan. "Why have they been loyal for so long? Just like for Maggie and Olivia, it must be because the details of the Tazza experience perfectly match what they are looking for. But many details that matter most to them seem to conflict with recent changes we've made. Take the job of 'feel part of the local community.' We heard many explanations for why Tazza was a great fit for this job: The crowd at any café was consistent enough that you could always count on seeing familiar faces. Some regulars were longtime locals, and that made others feel connected to the history and culture of the town outside the cafe—like they were locals too. This was reinforced by the distinct neighborhood decor of each cafe. And even new faces were mostly friendly ones.

"But now that we're trying to pull in on-the-go diners or business people, and using up valuable floor space for business meetings, the crowd is more variable—and transient. Less interested in meeting other people and really connecting to them. The environment becomes more generic with all the new additions to the menu and the layout, causing it to lose its local neighborhood feel. Regulars start leaving. And once a few leave, the crowd becomes less familiar, and it starts a chain reaction of departures."

This time Jordan summed up: "So explanation number two is: Tazza lost sight of what matters most to its best customers. That allowed critical elements of the experience to get lost as Tazza added all this other stuff to appeal to a broader set of people. You end up with a one-size-fits-none solution—and longtime customers leave."

"Excellent," Alex said. "These are both common market mystery patterns we see—especially for companies looking for new ways to grow. All that pressure to find new customers can result in a kind of organizational identity crisis."

"What do you mean?" asked Jordan.

"Think about it this way," said Alex. "Every organization, at any moment in time, is operating according to some set of assumptions about what business it's in. Assumptions about the customers it serves, how it serves them, who it competes against, how it competes, what outside forces matter, how it innovates, and so on. They might be stated assumptions, but more often they are unspoken ones that everyone just takes for granted.

"Either way, what matters most is *which* assumption is viewed as most important for defining the business. Some companies behave as if their *products* are primary and define themselves accordingly: 'We are in the car business,' 'We are in the insurance business,' and so on."

"In our case," said Jordan, "the parallel would be 'We are in the coffee business.'"

"Exactly," said Alex. "But that approach means you've fallen into, in your words, the Ptolemy trap—that's Ptrap with a *P*. It puts the wrong thing at the center of your model of reality, and makes it impossible to understand what's really happening around you or what to do about it. The goal becomes selling more products, even if it means drifting away from what made you successful in the first place: solving some set of customer jobs. Thus the organizational identity crisis.

"What's so useful about this map is that it shows the *actual* business—or businesses—that Tazza is in today, with customer jobs being a primary dimension. This is the key thing Cate and her team need to decide what business they want to be in going forward."

"Are these the messages we'll share with the leadership team?" Jordan asked.

"For sure," Alex replied. "But we need one more round of interpretation so they have what they need to make decisions. Ultimately that's why she asked us to do this investigation."

"What kind of decisions?"

"Put most simply, what things should Tazza start, stop, or continue doing to reach its goals. In this case, the team is looking to stop the revenue decline and get on a sustainable growth path. They need a plan for how to do that, and that means a set of decisions about where to focus the time, money, and assets of the company—and where not to focus."

Alex moved closer to the screen and pointed to the region where most of the check marks appeared.

"To that end, the last thing we should do is highlight which areas on the map are the best fit for Tazza—kind of like our home base within all this territory. I call it the *core market*. It's where we have a solution our customers love, that's better than the competition's, and that's aligned with our mission and identity."

Jordan quickly added one more highlighted block to the map. "I think it's this area here—jobs related to connection and entertainment, for people who live nearby and spend meaningful time in the cafe to solve for these jobs."

Market map for: *Tazza* — Circumstances / Jobs

Jobs \ Circumstances	Mike—Mobile worker	Amelia—Saturday night	Amelia—Late morning	The 3 Friends—Retired	Maggie—Early morning	Maggie—After workout	Olivia—After workout	On-the-go morning	On-the-go afternoon	On-the-go evening
Get work done—computer	✗		✓							
Get work done—meetings	✗									
Get work done—calls	✗									
Connect—Meet new people	✗	✗		✗						
Connect—Spend time with friends		✗		✓		✓	✓			
Connect—Feel close to family										
Connect—Feel part of the community				✓						
Be entertained—live music		✗								
Be entertained—games				✓						
Be entertained—watch sports				✗						
Maintain wellbeing—Have daily ritual					✓					
Maintain wellbeing—Get an energy boost					✓			✓	✓	✓
Maintain wellbeing—Take a break							✓	✓	✓	✓
Maintain wellbeing—Eat a snack								✗	✗	✗
Maintain wellbeing—Eat a healthy meal								✗	✗	✗

Labels on the map: *Office Oasis*, *O'Sullivan's*, *Tazza's "Core"*, *Santé*

Alex paused to process this, then agreed. "This picture is the main thing we need for the offsite. We'll share it with the team and tee up two questions: First, how to stabilize and grow in their core market? Assuming they agree with how we've defined it, of course. Second: Where else on the map should Tazza focus?"

Jordan, as usual, was already answering these questions in real time. "Seems like to grow the core we need to shift back to the experience we used to offer. Then find ways to make it even better—with a laser focus on the job specs for our core-market customers. Not sure how you answer the second question . . . the places we play outside the core don't seem very attractive based on this map."

"You may be right, though we can't know immediately. Attractive spots for Tazza have two characteristics," Alex explained. "They are *intrinsically* attractive because there are customers who have important, unsatisfied jobs, and there's a lot of value to capture for whichever company figures that out. Then these spots need to be attractive *to Tazza*, specifically, because it can create a great solution customers will love and that's better than the competition."

This explanation energized Jordan. "That will require some more analysis," she said enthusiastically, clearly excited by this prospect. "I can stay up tonight and get a first draft to you by tomorrow morning?"

"Jordan—it's Friday night. I'm so grateful for all your help—and for your incredible work ethic. But you should go home and take a break. Spend some time with Mark. You know people hire the relationships in their lives to get jobs done too, right? And these are the most important ones!"

"Wait . . . I hadn't thought about that. You mean you can apply this stuff to your personal life as well?"

"Of course—although your family might think you're nuts," Alex said with a laugh. "The language of jobs is really just a useful way to describe what people want out of life— their goals and dreams, problems they want to solve—large and small. Once you start looking through this lens, you see ways to apply it everywhere. Here's another example: We usually think it's just companies and other employers that hire people to work for them; but in fact people hire their employers to get jobs done in their lives too. And it might sound a little crazy to describe it this way, but by getting married, you and Mark are hiring each other to get a whole range of jobs done in your lives. What are they? And what does quality look like for solving them? I bet it doesn't include you working on a Friday night!"

Jordan sat processing this with her typical supercomputer facial expression. "Alex, you're kind of blowing my mind here. That's a pretty cool idea. For once, I have no immediate comment."

"Aha! This might just be the high point for me of our relationship so far. I asked questions that you couldn't answer! It's a first."

"Give me twenty-four hours." Jordan laughed. "I will get back to you."

17

WHY HIRE AN EMPLOYER?

The next morning was Saturday, and during breakfast Jordan relayed the events of the past week to her fiancé, Mark, a chronically sleep-deprived, third-year law student in the midst of an intensive season of job interviews. As she tried to explain the idea of understanding the jobs people are trying to get done as the main way to crack market mysteries, Mark just looked at her with confused, bleary eyes.

"Why do I hire coffee? I don't even drink coffee."

"Well, let's try another example—why hire a fiancée? What are you hiring me for as your life partner?"

"Um . . . I didn't realize you worked for me. If so, you're getting a bad deal; you make a lot more money and I'm just getting deeper in debt. You'd make more money from someone else. Also, this is getting weird."

"No! Let me explain. I don't mean literally hiring me to work for you. I'm using the word *hire* as a metaphor for why we consume things—like we consume products or services."

"Oh, that clears everything up. Now I'm a cannibal. Seriously, what are you talking about?" Mark was accustomed to Jordan breathlessly sharing her latest discoveries and interests, and equally familiar with taking a long time to catch up to her lightning-fast mind, a mind that could span a breadth of topics most people would find inconceivable. He loved this about her.

"OK, let me try one last example: You're in the middle of interviewing with a bunch of firms, looking for a job, right? And all those firms are evaluating you—and other candidates too, of course—and trying to decide who they should hire based on who is the best fit. All I'm saying is that's similar to what we do when we choose what products or services we buy, or solutions to adopt. Just like those law firms, we have jobs we need to get done. We have lots of these, all the time, and when they pop up, we look around for 'candidates'— products or other solutions—we might hire to get those jobs done. And we hire the solution that is the best fit for our job."

Jordan gestured toward her plate. "Like ten minutes ago I had the job of 'eat a healthy breakfast.' I opened the fridge to look for candidates I might hire, and settled on making this veggie egg-white breakfast scramble. I hired the scramble! This wouldn't always be my choice, but it is in this circumstance—it's Saturday morning, so I have time to cook it, and I'm going to work out soon, so I want to eat something with protein and other nutrients to give me energy."

Mark gave her a tired grin. "Hopefully these law firms are willing to 'hire a scramble' too, because scrambled is exactly how I feel these days . . . can't wait for this interview season to be over."

"Any of them would be lucky to have you," Jordan said. "And here's something to consider: It's not just that the firms are hiring you. *You* have jobs you're trying to get done too, for which you are looking to 'hire an employer.' A lot of them, actually. Functional jobs like making money to pay the bills or getting access to healthcare benefits. But also emotional jobs, like feeling inspired or like you're learning new things and growing. And social jobs, like being part of a community with shared values or purpose, or making a contribution to the world. So you're hiring an employer just as much as an employer is hiring you."

"That's an interesting way to look at it," Mark acknowledged. "I'd love to figure out what that list of jobs is for which I'm hiring a job . . . but I need to get ready to meet my study group. Can we put this on our list of things to talk about tonight at dinner?"

"Of course," Jordan replied with an affectionate gaze.

Once alone, Jordan idly stirred her breakfast and stared at the chaotic pattern that resulted. Although she was excited about the prior day's conclusions and believed they'd basically cracked the mystery, something was still bothering her. It still felt like some piece of the puzzle was missing.

She replayed in her mind what they'd learned so far. It was clear the Tazza experience had become too diluted, trying to be all things to all people and ending up as a one-size-fits-none solution. They'd lost sight of what mattered to their best customers, who understandably wandered away. It was equally clear Rob's programs were not only ineffective but making things worse, as they were alienating these same customers.

But was this all there was to the mystery? Had they gotten to the heart of it, or was there something else? And where, after all of the conversations they'd had, was the Mayor?

Jordan was grateful her first activity that morning was her Saturday spin class. The highlight of her week, it was filled with a mix of good friends and genial acquaintances and led by one of the most inspirational people she knew. There was nothing better than pushing herself physically while the pounding electronic music vibrated the clutter and worries out of her otherwise pristine mind. It often led to break-throughs on problems she was working on, and she hoped this would be the case as she grabbed her exercise bag and jogged out the door.

18

SPINNING

Jordan rushed into her spin studio still turning the Tazza case over in her mind. The studio was like a temple dedicated to the cause of collective perspiration, where each day highly trained spin instructors would lead hour-long rituals of stationary bike exertion. Jordan had discovered it right after moving from Michigan six months earlier, and just walking through the front door lifted her mood and energy level.

Small by midwestern standards, the studio had only two rooms dedicated to group classes, a warm-up area, and a juice bar named Polly's (after the owner's pet beagle). But it had quickly become her home away from home. Most people there were transplants of some sort, and this shared feeling of being uprooted made them feel all the more connected to these Saturday bonding experiences.

Jordan's best friend there was Marjory, a recent empty nester looking to retool for the digital economy by taking courses in computer programming. They'd struck up a friendship after Jordan offered to tutor her on the weekends. Marjory would usually arrive at class first, whirling in with the energy of a kid-liberated parent making up for lost time. They would spin side by side each week, then park at the juice bar to debrief on the workout, share stories of their personal lives, catch up on the latest reality TV show drama, and drink their favorite juices. Often their favorite instructor, Becky, would join them.

Jordan found Marjory in the warm-up area stretching out her hamstrings.

"Hey, Marjory! Ready for a big morning? I'm close to the halfway point on my quest. Thinking I can break it today—going to make Becky proud!"

"Quests" were individual programs Becky designed based on each person's health status and goals. Along with the adrenaline rush that came from spinning alongside others, Becky's exhortations to work harder, and the energizing music Becky carefully chose to accompany each stage of the workout, pursuing one's own quest was one of the most inspiring aspects of the whole experience.

When Marjory turned to see her, Jordan noticed something was amiss, as her normally upbeat demeanor was absent.

"Didn't you hear? Becky's not here today. She was supposed to have another two months to exercise before her pregnancy got too advanced to do this, but I guess she's having some complications so the doctor grounded her early. Nothing serious, she just wanted her to err on the safe side."

This bit of news hit Jordan with an emotional weight that surprised her. Of course they were all ecstatic Becky was going to be a mom for the first time, and health had to be the top priority. But Becky was the heart and soul of the studio. Not only did she motivate them to do more than they thought possible, she really cared about each of them. Jordan had even changed her schedule around on Thursday afternoons so she could do two classes a week with Becky after being disappointed by a few of the other instructors she'd tried.

"No, I didn't hear that," Jordan said, feeling dejected. "I mean, I hope she's OK—of course she should prioritize her baby and her health. But it won't be the same without her."

Suddenly the place seemed less like an inspiring arena where heroes pursued noble fitness quests and more like just another dive in a suburban strip mall looking out on an aging parking lot pockmarked with potholes.

"Yeah, I know," agreed Marjory. "It's going to be really hard to keep motivated without Becky here. I was kind of in denial about her going on maternity leave, but at least I thought I could remain in denial for another two months. I dunno, maybe we should look for someplace else? Better have a juice bar. If I can't discuss important topics like the latest reality TV episodes I will go insane."

Jordan felt deflated by this news, and the feeling was particularly acute given all the activity of the last two weeks. It had been exciting, but she realized how exhausting all the changes to her routine had been. And now here was this new disruption to adjust to.

Still, Marjory did her best to rally her. "Anyway, let's muddle through the workout. We can still see Becky:—she organized a group to take me out for brunch after this for my birthday—you should come. Can't believe she remembered! Even my kids forgot. There's a new bistro just opened over on State Street, supposedly the eggs Benedict is to die for. Then we're thinking about going to a movie over—"

"Wait!" Jordan interrupted. "Marjory—what did you say?"

"There's a new bistro—name is Florio's or Cheerio's or something like that."

"No! I mean before that."

"Um . . . the spin class is taking me out for my birthday?"

"Yes . . . of course . . . Marjory . . . that's it! I see what we've been missing this whole time!"

Marjory was used to odd behavior from Jordan, but she usually chalked it up to Jordan's brain existing on a higher dimension than the average mortal's. This time, however, she wondered if Jordan had lost it.

"Jordan—what on earth are you talking about?"

"Sorry, Marjory—can't stay for class. I have to go. I think I know where the Mayor is!"

Jordan grabbed her gym bag and rushed out the door, leaving Marjory standing alone and thoroughly perplexed. As she watched Jordan leave, she shouted after her, "Who's the Mayor?"

19

THE OFFSITE

The Prescott House on Cape Cod was an early twentieth-century summer mansion built by a long-deceased magnate that now hosted conferences and weddings. Less opulent than its Gilded Age cousins farther south in Newport, it nevertheless boasted forty guest rooms and a wide lawn sloping down to the ocean that could comfortably field two simultaneous football games. Only an hour's drive from Boston, the spot barely qualified as on Cape Cod, located on the peninsula's inner elbow, just southeast of the flexed bicep where the Pilgrims landed centuries earlier. While its founder had thoughtfully protected the surrounding acreage as an ecological preserve, Alex couldn't help thinking this magnanimous gesture diminished by the presence on this land of Prescott's own tomb. But after the scenic morning drive down through early spring foliage mottled with flooded cranberry bogs, he was prepared to let gratitude to Mr. Prescott carry the day.

Massimo, who Alex encountered in the lobby when he arrived, was less charitable.

"A tomb! Who needs their own tomb? Back in Italy we have a saying—*Alla fine del gioco, re e pedone finiscono nella stessa scatola.* Once the game is over, the king and the pawn end up in the same box."

By nine o'clock, the rest of the team had converged from their Boston suburbs. After fueling up with a continental breakfast, they took their seats around a large oval conference table in what was once the Prescott family sitting room, now adapted with the tools of a modern office environment.

Cate kicked things off by introducing the less familiar faces in the room.

"Thanks all for being here today. We have important work to do, so I appreciate your full engagement. Before we start I'd like to introduce some special guests who might be new to some of you. First we have two of our board members here, Ethan Raynor and Katrina Romero. And this is Henry Durant, the senior executive from Clarity Bank who is leading our IPO. Great to have you all here today."

All three responded with silent, solemn head nods, and Cate continued.

"We have one objective today: to align on how we'll achieve our growth goals over the next year. We are at a turning point in our company's history, and it's essential that we have a clear plan we are all committed to. The decisions we make will determine where we focus our resources for the remaining half of the fiscal year—which includes the time horizon for the IPO less than two months from now."

The team listened attentively, with occasional glances at Henry the banker, as if hoping to get some indication of his state of mind. They all knew he was there to assess Tazza's future—and them—and that today could make or break the IPO.

"Rob, I know you've been working with the team to prepare updates on our new growth initiatives, and we're looking forward to hearing about them. First, though, we're going to hear from Alex Baker. As you know, we hired Alex to gather some fresh insights on our customers and market position. He'll share a summary of his findings so we are all working from the same fact base. Alex, the floor is yours."

Alex stood and walked to the front of the room while an assistant loaded his presentation on the communal laptop.

"Thanks, Cate. Good morning, everyone. It's a privilege to be here and hopefully to help in some small way as you tackle these important issues. Before I start, I'd like to acknowledge the fantastic help I've had over the past few weeks from one of your colleagues, Jordan Sims. She's not here today, but none of this would have been possible without her. I'm sure you know this, but you're very lucky to have her."

So lucky, thought Rob. *I'll be having a conversation with Jordan very soon.*

"This morning I'll share the findings from the investigation we did into Tazza's current market position, customers, and competitors. As Cate might have mentioned, our approach was a bit unconventional, so I'll start with some background on how we went about it."

Alex quickly shared the minimum required background on how he and Jordan had conducted their investigation, including the language, method, and key tools they'd used. When this was finished, he pulled up a slide with the final map they'd developed. Methodically, he talked the group through what they'd learned about why Tazza was hired, why it was fired, and where Tazza and its main competitors played today.

As Alex spoke, Rob listened with increasing irritation. He wasn't about to let people get the impression he didn't already understand what was happening in the market. But when he finally spoke, he chose his words carefully.

"Thanks, Alex. This is very interesting. But if I'm reading your map correctly, it seems you've confirmed the value of our move into several new product categories. Those places on the map where competitors are focused, outside what you've called our core—those are exactly the areas I pushed the organization to move into six months ago as new opportunities for growth."

Rob felt particularly satisfied he'd managed to remind everyone these initiatives were his idea while seeming to use Alex's own findings to justify them.

"Not exactly," Alex replied. "This map is primarily a view of the jobs customers are trying to get done, who they hire to solve for them, and where different competitors are focused. Based on our research, customers prefer other solutions to

Tazza outside of your core market—though it certainly doesn't mean you can't win there in the future."

Rob couldn't let this go unchallenged. "Of course we are not yet winning in those markets—we just launched our programs and they need time to show results. It's kind of naive to expect that to happen overnight."

"I agree," said Alex. "These things always take time. The question for you to consider is what more time is likely to reveal. You have the most recent performance data as well, which I'm sure will help in your planning."

At that Rob was silent, as he was not eager, at the moment, to focus on these numbers. Alex, for his part, had no desire to antagonize Rob further. Having long since mastered the art of conference table diplomacy, he pivoted smoothly to his summary comments.

"But Rob raises what I believe is *the* central question for you all to grapple with today: What business do you want to be in? I can't answer this question for you, nor can any amount of analysis. It's something every leadership team needs to debate, decide on, and refine over time. My one piece of advice, though, is this: Answer it from the perspective of customer jobs to be done. Don't define your business by the products you sell, or by your business model, or by some set of customer characteristics. Define your business by the customer jobs you exist to solve, and let that be your North Star.

"If you get clarity on these, many other things will fall into place. All your energies will be focused on what ultimately drives any business's success: Creating value for customers. You'll see clearly who you are competing against, and what it takes to win. Previously inexplicable shifts and disruptions in the world around you will start to make more sense. Most importantly, it will align everyone who works at Tazza behind an inspiring sense of purpose—and guide them to make customer-centric decisions every day.

"Although no one can answer this question for you, this map gives you a great set of clues for where to start. For most of your history, your choice—whether conscious or not—has been this area here, what we've highlighted as Tazza's core market. Your extraordinary success has been in creating an environment that fosters a sense of community for customers, even a kind of second home, with great attention to the details that matter most to them. Things like a local flavor, familiar faces, spacious surroundings, support for activities, and so on."

"That seems kind of obvious," Rob interrupted. "And we still serve those needs today. Why would it change? If anything, we now offer those same customers even more—with more ways to generate revenue."

The rest of the team had stayed silent as the meeting turned into a two-person dialogue. The banker looked particularly keen to hear Alex's answer.

"It's true that some cafes are still doing well—the ones where the experience is still optimized for those community seekers. But elsewhere it appears the beloved Tazza experience has been diluted by trying to solve for a much broader set of customer jobs—causing many of your most loyal customers to leave."

Rob had started the morning feeling irritated, but now felt defensive as well. "Alex, this is interesting, but I don't think we'll be able to make decisions about where to invest for growth based on just a handful of in-person interviews you've done."

"I agree numbers are important, so a great next step would be to validate some of these observations more generally," Alex said. "But based on my experience over the past twenty years, these findings are highly likely to hold up. And what I would *not* do is make big strategic decisions that conflict with these results."

"Well, it seems to me that until we do that, we're not really better off than we were a few weeks ago," argued Rob. "In contrast, I'm looking forward to sharing real data on our growth initiatives."

The room was silent while the group weighed both sides of what seemed to be an impasse. Everyone looked at Cate, and Rob noticed that Henry Durant was watching her closely. The team knew Cate would be decisive, but just as she was about to speak, the door opened and Jordan burst into the room, out of breath.

"Hi, everyone! Really sorry to interrupt your meeting. It's just that I have some new information to share that I think you should hear. Oh hi, Alex!"

Alex smiled and waved from the end of the room.

"Um . . . OK, I guess this is a little awkward. Sorry, Cate—first time I've been in a meeting like this, you know?

I just thought you should hear what I've learned about why Tazza is losing customers. Is that OK?"

Rob responded before anyone else could. "Jordan, we're rather busy at the moment. This is an executive strategy offsite, and Alex has done a fine job of sharing the work that you and he developed. It's all very interesting, but we're about to move on to discussing our strategic options and which of the many growth initiatives I've been leading are the ones to double down on."

Before Jordan could protest, Ethan Raynor spoke for the first time. "I'd like to hear what she has to say. We have time. Jordan, please, go ahead."

"Oh thank you, sir! OK. I guess you've already heard from Alex. Where to begin? The thing is, Alex and I learned a ton about customers by talking to them directly—so much fun too! Highly recommend it. But something kept bugging me—like we were missing something right in front of us. I didn't figure it out until I was at spin class this past Saturday morning talking to my friend Marjory . . . well, I guess that sounds crazy but I can explain."

Based on the group's expressions, it was safe to say that it did, indeed, sound crazy. Only Alex and Cate seemed to think otherwise.

"That's when it hit me: We spent most of our time focused on why people hired Tazza in the first place, and then what they liked—or didn't like—about the experience there. We heard some great ideas for how it could be improved, and, crucially, learned why people were *firing* Tazza and causing our sales decline. But there was one thing we overlooked—a detail so fundamental to the Tazza experience that once it was gone, people left in droves."

"What was it, Jordan? What was it that changed? What was missing?" asked James, who was looking intently at her.

Jordan returned his gaze, then said simply, "You, James. You were missing."

20

CONNECTING DOTS

A long silence fell over the room as the group tried to grasp the meaning of Jordan's surprising assertion. Even Rob found himself eager to hear more, and even Alex was unsure where this was headed.

"I can explain," said Jordan, finally starting to catch her breath. "Remember, James, when we came to speak to you in Providence? We asked why sales there had turned around in the past three months. You said it was likely because of the corporate partnership program—SIP—which you launched during that time, and all the success your team had signing up new corporate accounts. But you hadn't measured the results yet, so I went back to my database and checked. Almost none of the traffic to Providence came from those partnerships.

"So there was still this puzzle of why things had turned around. And it stayed a puzzle until my spin class. You see, I've been going there twice a week since I moved here six months ago. I love it. It's been this kind of anchor of stability during a year of so many changes—new city, new job, getting married. I mean I'm excited to get married, but all the planning, pressure from relatives . . . It's been a lot to handle. But spin class would recharge and inspire me, every time.

"Until this past Saturday. That's when I learned my long-time instructor, Becky, was going on maternity leave and wouldn't be back for at least a year. I was happy for her—but sad for me! It surprised me how crushed I felt. Why would her leaving have such an impact? Everything else about the place was the same—same people, same workout, same music, same yummy juice-bar drinks. But Becky was what made it special. She really cared about each of us. She made the effort to understand our goals and dreams, help us create plans to achieve them, and figure out how to motivate us to stick to those plans. She even found ways to connect us to each other. Before long we cared as much about each other's success as we did about our own. Like we were a team—it made it even more inspiring.

"That's why it hit me so hard when she was no longer there. It just wasn't the same, and I haven't felt like going back since."

Rob was getting impatient. "This is a touching story, Jordan, but what does any of this have to do with Tazza?"

"Good question," Jordan replied. "I didn't see the connection until my friend Marjory mentioned Becky was taking her out for her birthday. 'I can't believe she even remembered,' she said. That reminded me of something that happened when we met James in Providence. There was a woman there with her husband—it was her birthday that day. Remember, James? You had one of the baristas create a special latte with her age etched into the foam. It was such a nice, personal gesture—it showed how much you cared. And that's *exactly* the kind of thing Becky would do! I mean not exactly: I don't think she can do latte art—that looks hard, you know? But she made those little caring, personal gestures all the time."

Cate smiled proudly at this anecdote and gave James a warm glance.

"Then it struck me," Jordan continued. "Maybe the reason sales turned around in Providence was not because the partnership program started—it was simply because James *himself* relocated there. Once he arrived he couldn't help but re-create the same caring atmosphere that has long been the hallmark of the Tazza experience. He role modeled it, and taught the other baristas how important it was. James is just like Becky. She's more than just an instructor, and he's more than just a barista. He's the heart and soul of the cafe and the experience it provides.

"Once I had that insight, a bunch of things started making more sense. Like the fact that James leaving the North End Tazza also coincided with the start of its more dramatic sales decline. And I remembered that a customer named Nicole had all these nice things to say about him. I went back to my notes from that day. She said James would listen to her complain about her dating life, that he introduced her to her current boyfriend, and even found someone to rent a room in her home. All these were touches just for her—including connecting her with other people in the community.

"Then there was Barb, the person who fired Tazza . . . She described a bunch of things that had changed about Tazza that caused her to leave. But what's one important thing she found at her country club? Her coach, Liam! She raved about him, and when he dropped by he also made a nice personal gesture when he gave her the number of a physical therapist—not for her, but for her daughter."

"Jordan—are you saying our entire sales decline was caused by a single barista changing jobs and moving to a new location?" Kelly asked.

"No—nothing that extreme. I think what happened was we didn't fully understand *why* our best customers were hiring us—and that one of the most essential elements of the Tazza experience was the role baristas play. Not just James, but all of them. What else happened around the time James changed roles? We had high turnover in our barista staff, so there were a lot of new people. Normally they'd go through the training program James had started, and they would come on board knowing the Tazza way of doing things. But as James told us, he'd had to put that program on hold because of all the work for the other growth initiatives. But what was the one place he'd resurrected the program?"

"At the Providence location," James answered. "It's true that I don't have much time anymore to supervise the training program," he sighed, finally voicing a long-standing frustration.

"This rings true for me, Jordan," said Cate. "Caring about each person and connecting dots to create a community—that's exactly what Marco did back in Italy in that little Florence cafe that inspired Tazza. I guess we started taking that for granted in our own cafes, losing sight of what was most important to our customers."

Rob, who had been having trouble staying silent, finally interrupted. "So are you saying that everything Alex has been telling us is wrong?"

Alex wondered if Rob hoped this was the case.

"No," Jordan said. "All the things Alex described are still really important. But we have to understand *all* the reasons our customers hire us. I even went back and ran some numbers to look at the sales decline in our fourteen locations relative to the level of turnover in the barista staff. There was a strong correlation. So it's like we start to dilute the experience with all these other things, and then we lose some of the most important elements, and suddenly Tazza isn't special anymore."

Rob could see where this was heading, but wasn't ready to give up on his programs yet. "This is all just surmising. We need hard data—and statistically significant data—to evaluate all these things."

"I agree that data is valuable," said Jordan. "No one loves it more than me—I've been immersed in it all my life. But hearing from customers directly is just as important—especially early on. 'Small data before big data,' we say. It even helped me figure out the answer to another big puzzle I couldn't get out of my head."

"What's that, Jordan?" Cate asked.

"Where the Mayor went!"

"Seriously? I suggest we move on to the next phase of work," Rob said. "Speculating on why the Mayor left and where he went is not helpful at this point."

"We don't have to speculate," Jordan said. "We can hear the Mayor's words directly—he's right outside."

She walked to the side door and opened it. "I'd like to introduce you to Ed Amato—a.k.a. the Mayor. Ed, come on in."

21

THE MAYOR

E d looked sheepish as he entered but turned joyful when half the room stood to embrace him in a warm, extended reunion. There were tears in his eyes when Cate gave him the longest hug of the group.

"Ed—so wonderful to see you after all this time!" Cate exclaimed. "Jordan, how did you find him?"

Everyone settled back into their chairs, with Ed at the head of the table, as Jordan explained.

"Once I realized how important the baristas were, I asked myself, 'What else could Ed hire to get that same experience?' Then I remembered Barb's coach, Liam, had seen Ed at the New England Ultras soccer supporters' event—and even coached Ed at one of their amateur games. At the time we didn't think the Ultras scene could really be a competitor to Tazza—it was just so different it couldn't possibly appeal to Tazza's core customers. But that should have been a clue right there! Ed had so thoroughly vanished that, *wherever* he was, there *couldn't* be much overlap between his new crowd and the old one. He simply had to be hiring something entirely different."

"If that's the case, then why would it even appeal to Ed?" Massimo asked.

"It didn't, entirely. It was loud, and crazy, and not nearly as conducive to the intimate conversations Ed loves so much. But the amateur team had the one big thing that mattered most to Ed and that he'd lost at Tazza: someone who cared about his life, invested time in it, and took pains to build a community of people who looked out for each other. After all, that's what a team is, right? It made the not-so-great aspects secondary. I decided to go to a game on Sunday afternoon and found the supporters' section—and there was Ed!"

Jordan turned to Ed. "He graciously agreed to come today—and he should really be the one to tell his story."

Ed hesitated, but didn't take long to live up to his garrulous reputation.

"Thanks, Jordan. Gosh . . . I feel overwhelmed. What a lovely reunion with all of you. I realize how much I've missed you all. It's just wonderful to see everyone.

"I suppose I should first apologize for disappearing like I did. I thought about coming in to say hi many times, but I just felt guilty about leaving and then life got so busy I never got around to it. Plus, so many of the faces at Tazza had changed that I didn't think I'd know anyone anymore."

"Why *did* you leave, Ed?" James asked.

"Well . . . you know I love Tazza. Always have. Was like home for me for so many years, and couldn't imagine life without it. Then things started to change—small things at first. New decor, food, drinks—not a big deal, just started to feel less warm and more businesslike somehow. But then the crowd started to change too. Don't get me wrong—I'm happy for Tazza when it gets more customers. But the new people seemed less interested in making conversation, and more just absorbed in their phones or computers. Or they'd be working, or having meetings. One guy actually got mad at me when I tried chatting with him at the coffee bar. Told me to buzz off and mind my own business.

"Then the baristas started changing too. They're all nice kids, of course—sorry, I call anyone under the age of fifty 'kid'—but seemed more formal, not as interested in chatting with other folks. And they put a conference room where we used to watch the soccer games! I guess when James left, it felt like it was time for a change. My doctor had been warning me to get off my seat and start moving around more. So I called an old friend who was part of this Ultras group. He introduced me to the coach there, and the club they go to before and after the games. In some ways it gave me what the old Tazza used to—a community of people, a coach who seemed to care about me and helped me out, even feeling like part of a team.

"I have to say, though, it's nowhere close to what we had at Tazza. For starters, the coffee is awful. I mean just awful! Then it's a bit hard for me to get to—I can't just walk down the street, I have to take the train out of town. And with all due respect to my doctor, I enjoy sitting on my rear and chatting with people! More than anything I miss all of you.

Especially you, Cate—and you, James. When Jordan came up to me on Sunday and said I could see everyone again today, I jumped at the chance."

"I'm glad you did," said Cate. "Not only is it wonderful to see you, but you've helped us see how we've drifted from what's been the core of our identity—and our success—for so long. Tazza has always been in the business of helping people connect and create communities. I'm committed to getting back to that, whatever the consequences are. That's what we are all about."

To everyone's surprise, Henry Durant stood and spoke. "Ed, a pleasure to meet you—and thank you for sharing your story. Cate, it's clear your company has a deep connection to its customers. My advice to the team is to cherish this. We bankers get a bad rap, but in my firm we cherish our customers as well—and that means doing whatever we can to help them realize their dreams. In your case, helping you grow and create something that can touch the lives of many more people. Everyone, I think I've seen enough. Good luck with the rest of your offsite. I'm looking forward to a successful IPO!"

With that, he exited. Everyone felt elated. Everyone except for Rob, who looked defeated. Cate noticed this immediately, and intervened with her usual deft touch.

"Congratulations, everyone! Let's get to work and focus on moving forward. Rob, we still need to cover all of these new growth initiatives. I can see many ways to make use of the great capabilities you've built. That will be our task this afternoon—for now let's break for lunch."

As the group dispersed, Kelly and Massimo approached Jordan to congratulate her.

"Amazing work, Jordan," Kelly said. "You clearly made a strong impression on Cate and Henry both—and on me. Who would have thought the key to securing our IPO would be a twenty-three-year-old computer genius?"

Jordan beamed at this praise, and Massimo added, "You know what they say in my country? *La barba non fa il filosofo.* The beard does not make the philosopher. Well done, my friend!"

EPILOGUE

SIX MONTHS LATER

B ack where it all began," Alex said to Cate, as they sat together at the North End Tazza coffee bar.

The place was as busy as ever, but Alex noticed a few changes from his last visit. What used to be an empty conference room was now full of people glued to a reinstalled bank of widescreen televisions. A loud cheer came from the room, and Alex noticed Ed yelling enthusiastically at the screen in Italian. The Mayor, apparently, was back, as were his beloved soccer matches.

"Yes," Cate agreed. "Where it *really* all began—we've been trying to get back to what made Tazza special in the first place."

"How have you done that?" Alex asked. "Besides getting Ed back his soccer games."

Cate laughed. "It's true that part of the solution was just adding back some of the pieces of the experience we'd lost— like Ed's games—and Ed himself of course! And we put

James back in charge of the barista training. The IPO was a success and gave us the resources to invest in a bunch of new programs that help us solve the core jobs of our customers better. For example, the 'meet new people' job made sense for us, so we transformed our corporate partnership program into something called the Tazza Social Club. The focus is not on business networking but on organizing meetup events at our cafes. It's been a hit with corporate customers because it helps employees new to the area meet others and feel connected to the local community."

"That's great," Alex said. "And totally aligned with your core market focus."

"For sure. Interestingly, many of the capabilities we built for our former growth initiatives turned out to be useful— like the ones for the corporate partnership program. We were just focusing on the wrong jobs to be done. Even the Connoisseurs' Club database has proved useful—it's the natural list of people to market the social club and other programs to."

"That reminds me—whatever happened to Rob?"

"He stayed for a couple of months after the offsite, then decided to go back to the beverage company he came from. Doing well, I hear. He's a good guy—has a lot of strengths, but was a bit too conventional in his thinking. And as I said, the capabilities he helped build are still valuable."

"Yeah, I can see that," said Alex. "All that stuff is not intrinsically good or bad; it just has to be pointed in the right direction."

Cate nodded. "Another cool thing that came from your research—this was Jordan's idea—is that we launched this idea of 'rent-a-table' memberships. It's for people who just want to hang out here for some period of time, and not feel guilty about having to buy food or drinks they don't want. They can sign up for a membership subscription, and they get benefits including the ability to reserve specific tables. The students and the game players love it, of course. And surprisingly, they end up actually buying more in the cafes! We think it's because they end up spending even more time there.

"We preserved part of the original corporate partnership program—but we pivoted it away from generic partners toward companies that share our community-building values. The New England Soccer League, for example. They've sent tons of people here, and we're now catering their events and providing coffee to them. We even found a way to work with Office Oasis to remedy their coffee situation. Another of Jordan's great ideas."

As if on cue, Jordan approached the bar to join them.

"Jordan!" Cate called out. "So nice to see you. How's the new job?"

"Oh hi, Cate—it's fantastic! I'm leading two new market investigations already. Check out my new business card."

The card said "Jordan Sims, Market Detective" just below the logo of Alex's firm.

"Congratulations, Jordan. And to you too, Alex. Can't believe you stole her from me."

"Neither can I," agreed Alex. "But it's my good fortune. She's already introduced a number of innovations into how we do things. Says she's going to bring our market detective agency into the modern age."

"True," Jordan said. "The directed–data mining algorithms I'm developing will make things much more efficient. I've managed to connect them to the tools I built for collecting the small data from our market investigations. I think this will really accelerate this new case we're working on. You know, the one I'm calling 'The Case of the California Tea Cabal'?"

"Indeed. You have a flair for naming things, Jordan," said Cate. "Well, let's drink up! As Massimo would say, *Chi ha amico, è ricco*. Who has friends is rich."

The three laughed and looked out on the horizon, where a lone sailboat moved steadily with a strong wind at its back. Clinking their coffee cups, they drank deeply, toasting to smooth sailing ahead.

PART II

Becoming a Market Detective

The story of how Jordan, Alex, and Cate solved the mystery of Tazza's disappearing customers illustrates a powerful set of techniques that can be applied in a wide variety of real-world market investigations. I'll now step out of the Tazza story and explain how.

I'll start by focusing on the most fundamental—and in my view, the most important—type of customer interaction: a direct conversation between two people. It's often the single most valuable and efficient source of insights, and the one that anyone can (and should!) learn to use. I also think of it as the "atomic unit" of techniques for understanding customers: if you master the required language, method, and mindset, you then have a strong foundation for many other techniques. These include traditional approaches, like in-depth interviews, focus groups, surveys, and observation, as well as more recent, big data–inspired methods.

While the Tazza story revolved around one of the most commonly occurring market mysteries, the value of talking to real, live human beings extends to just about any type of market mystery that comes along. These include:

- *Innovation challenges*, such as serving existing customers better, attracting new ones, or creating entirely new products and services;
- *Strategic challenges*, such as finding attractive new markets to pursue, identifying new businesses to create, or determining how to respond to a rapidly changing environment;
- *Marketing challenges*, such as creating messages that really resonate or finding effective ways to segment markets; and
- *Organizational challenges*, such as aligning an organization around a common purpose, inspiring its people, or communicating its mission to the outside world.

Finally, it's the skill set that can help entire organizations turn the rhetoric of customer-centricity into reality. Consider the value of *everyone* in your organization being empowered to have insightful, mutually rewarding conversations with the customers they serve—whether internal or external. How much of a difference would it make? For most organizations, it would be a huge step towards realizing their aspiration of putting customers at the center of everything they do.

So without further ado, let's dive in.

(And for more information on how to apply the ideas of this book across a range of market mysteries, please visit www.marketdetective.com.)

Understanding Customers: The Fundamentals

Imagine you set out to have a conversation with a complete stranger with the aim of understanding, at a deep level, that person's aspirations and challenges in some area of life. Your motive is noble: you want to find ways to help.

How would you go about doing this?

A moment's reflection raises several questions: What would you say first? Assuming they agreed to talk to you, what questions would you ask? How would you guide the conversation to discover something useful? How would you capture and interpret what you're learning so it can inspire ways you might help that person? Importantly, how would you do all that in a way that is empathetic, honest, and leaves you both feeling like it was a great use of time?

Confidently leading such conversations toward a productive, mutually satisfying outcome requires the aspiring market detective to learn three things:

- A *language* that defines what information you're looking for
- A *method* for discovering, organizing, and interpreting that information
- A *mindset* that maximizes your chances of doing so

Because the language is the foundation for the other topics, I'll start there.

The Language of Customer Centricity

Every craft has its own peculiar language that practitioners speak and understand. Physicians talk about chronic and acute conditions, inpatients and outpatients, morbidities and comorbidities, and so on. Lawyers enthuse about civil and criminal law, injunctions, actions, torts, and a host of other things opaque to the uninitiated. Accountants expound on debits, credits, cash flows, balance sheets, and income statements. Each language consists of its own specialized vocabulary, along with rules for how the words in it relate to one another.

So it should be with the craft of the market detective. However, unlike in the case of doctors, lawyers, or accountants, there is no standard, widely accessible language to guide interactions with customers. Instead, what exists tends to be either the purview of highly trained specialists or, at the opposite extreme, too vague and ambiguous to be useful. Even more problematic, many existing approaches guide investigators to ask the wrong questions, generating vast quantities of data and analysis about things that may not even really matter.

What's needed is a language that guides us to *ask the right questions* which lead to the *right kinds of insights* at the *right level of detail.* The right questions are those that help us discover what really matters to customers: the problems they most want to solve, the goals they most want to achieve—the jobs they most want to get done. Identifying these jobs is foundational, as they are the root cause underlying *why* customers choose and behave as they do. Once we discover these jobs, our questions then need to help us understand them with enough richness of detail to create products, services, and experiences that perfectly solve for them. All these requirements are met by the language I'll describe here.

To introduce it, I'll work through an example drawn from the Tazza story: that of Amelia, the young woman sitting in a cafe after class doing her schoolwork. Imagine you are in the role of either Jordan or Alex, working on behalf of Tazza to better understand its customers. What is it you want to learn about Amelia? The answer to this question forms the vocabulary of our language.

First, you want to know the *circumstance* she is in. Circumstance is the relevant context of someone's life that you want to understand in a market investigation. It can be characterized by a range of factors, some relatively narrow (such as where the person is or what they're doing), and some broader and more enduring (such as family status or personal values). Here are some useful categories of circumstance to explore and how they might look for Amelia.

- *Situational*: The factors that define where someone is in time and space, answering such questions as where the person is located, when they're there, who they are with, and what they are doing. In some cases, the answers will be confined to a relatively narrow duration and location. This is true for Amelia, where we're most interested in her situational circumstance of "in the cafe, late morning after class, alone." However, depending on what you're interested in, you might want to characterize someone's circumstance over a longer period of time in their life or across a broader geography.

- *Demographic*: Variables such as family status, financial status, life stage, living situation, and so on. For Amelia, we might list things like "early twenties, single, lives with roommates, student."

- *Identity*: Factors such as personal values, attitudes, beliefs, and affiliations. For Amelia, this could include things like "is close to her family, goal-oriented, hard-working."

- *Agency*: Variables that define who the *primary focus* of the conversation is. Most often it is the person you're talking with. But it could be someone the person you're talking to has responsibility for—for example, the child of a parent you're interviewing, or the elderly parents of an adult child. For Amelia it's straightforward, as we're just interested in understanding Amelia herself.

The concept of circumstance plays two important roles. First, it helps establish boundaries around a subset of a customer's life; without them your efforts will be so undefined that they're unlikely to result in anything useful. These boundaries define the *field of vision* on which you'll focus your market investigation lens. How broad or narrow this field of vision is depends on what type of problem—or mystery—you are trying to solve. For example, the boundaries could be very narrow (zoomed in) and focused on a tiny slice of someone's life—say, standing in line at the grocery store. Or the boundaries could be broader (zoomed out) and focused on a longer time period—say, the duration of someone's home-buying journey, which might be months or even years. In this latter case, the single customer interaction we're contemplating here might be just one of many we explore across a longer customer journey.

Second, a clear view of the relevant circumstance is essential for a full understanding of the *other* things we'd like to know about a customer, as they are all *relative* to the circumstance that customer is in. With Amelia, we are primarily interested in the jobs she is trying to get done within the relatively narrow circumstance of "in the cafe after class." However, even within that context there are broader factors—such as where she is in her life and what type of person she is—that influence how she evaluates potential solutions for her jobs.

This is a good segue to the next thing we'd like to know about Amelia: *the jobs she wants to get done.* The second element of our language, a job can be either a *problem* someone is trying to solve or a *goal* someone is trying to achieve. In either case, jobs provide the motivation and energy a customer needs to explore potential solutions, embrace some of them, and reject others. As in the case of circumstance, there are several useful categories of jobs to explore.

- *Functional* jobs: practical goals to achieve or problems to solve. For Amelia, these include "complete my
  schoolwork," "get into medical school," and "stay alert
  and energized."
- *Emotional* jobs: emotional states you want to experience
  or avoid (typically either positive emotional states to at-
  tain or negative ones to avoid or overcome). Amelia's
  emotional jobs might include "reduce stress of chal-
  lenging courses" or "feel optimistic about my future."
- *Social* jobs: how you want to be perceived by or engage with others. For Amelia, these could include
  "stay connected to my family," "spend time with my
  friends," or "meet new people."

Once again, you can see the interrelationships between
the elements of our language. The jobs someone is trying to
get done are always *relative* to a particular circumstance—
and there is usually a whole "bundle" of jobs the person is
trying to solve for, simultaneously, in that circumstance. In
the case of Amelia, her main job was "complete schoolwork,"
but we learned she also wants to "stay connected to family"
as she sits in the cafe. Your objective in a market investigation is to not only uncover individual jobs, but understand
the bundles customers are trying to solve for, simultaneously,
in a given circumstance. This is one way you can capture suf-
ficient detail to innovate complete, nuanced experiences that
are rich in features that really matter.

This leads us to the next topics of interest about Amelia:
what she's currently hiring (if anything) to get these jobs done and

how she evaluates the quality of potential solutions. Expanding on our jobs metaphor, we say that people "hire" products or services to get jobs done in their lives—just like you might hire a person for a job like babysitting the kids or fixing the plumbing. Understanding what's being hired today—and why—is essential information if you're looking for ways to serve them better. Of course, if they are not currently hiring anything, that's important to know too.

Amelia is clearly hiring the Tazza cafe to solve for many of the jobs listed above. However, we learned there are other things she has hired for those jobs. For example, for the "get schoolwork done" job she sometimes hires the library or her dorm or a quiet spot in one of the campus classroom buildings. For the "meet new people" job (for which Tazza was not a great solution), she sometimes hires a bar or a concert or a club.

This illustrates how powerful the jobs lens can be for revealing who your real competition is in a market—and it often doesn't look anything like your organization or what you're selling today. For example, we might have thought the competition for Amelia's Tazza coffee purchases would be limited to other coffee shops, or perhaps other ways to obtain a cup of coffee, such as making it in her dorm or going to her campus's dining hall. But once we understand the jobs she hires Tazza for, you can see the actual competition includes solutions that have nothing to do with selling or consuming coffee.

Current solutions and how a customer evaluates their quality are intimately related; by exploring either one you'll typically learn a lot about the other. When doing so, you want to determine how the *customer* defines a quality solution—not how you or your company would define it. This is so important it bears repeating: it's the customer's definition of high quality that matters, not yours. The world is full of innovations offering features and benefits their *creators* were excited about but that *customers* ignored or rejected. The way to avoid this is to understand what really matters from your customer's perspective, including:

- *Criteria used to assess "job candidates"*: we typically apply a number of criteria when evaluating the suitability of potential solutions for a job. Cost is almost always one of them, but there are usually others such as convenience, ease of use, or ease of integration with a current routine. In the case of Amelia, the proximity of Tazza to her late-morning organic chemistry class was an important reason she chose it. Other criteria will be very specific to the job and circumstance of interest. For example, Amelia valued the buzz of background noise that helped her concentrate and the relative anonymity that prevented interruptions.

- *What good, bad, and great look like for each of these criteria*: besides the criteria themselves, you want to understand what level of performance corresponds to a great solution, a good one, and a bad one. Take Amelia's "buzz of background noise" consideration: presumably if it was too loud, it would be impossible to concentrate, and it would be similar if the noise was too soft. There is an ideal level she's looking for on this dimension.

- *Trade-offs they want (or are willing) to make*: since we can't always have "great" on every dimension that matters, it's important to understand what trade-offs customers are willing to make—for example, how much more they are willing to pay for an improvement in performance on other evaluative criteria.

- *Essential features of the experience*: even though customers can't always tell us exactly what they want in a solution (that's your job to figure out!), they often share specific ideas for what they'd like to see included in it. For example, although Amelia was pretty happy with the overall Tazza experience, she called out her desire for additional outlets to power her laptop and open up more places she could park in the cafe while she did her schoolwork.

Finally, there is one more thing we'd like to understand about Amelia: *the help wanted signs*. These are indicators that, whatever solutions may be available, there are still opportunities to create and provide better ones. They also provide a great deal of information about *how* to go about doing that. Help wanted signs manifest in four scenarios:

1. *No existing solution*: there might simply be no solution, anywhere, that solves for the job to be done. In this case, the existence of these important, unsatisfied jobs *is* the help wanted sign.

2. *Existing solutions, but barriers in the way that need to be overcome*: solutions might exist for the job, but some barrier is getting in the way of the customer hiring them. For example, the solutions might be too expensive (wealth barrier), impossible to physically access (access barrier), or too complex to use (skills barrier). In this case, the barriers are the help wanted signs.

3. *Existing solutions, but they are low quality*: the solutions are poor ones *relative to how the customer defines quality*. This could mean either that existing solutions perform poorly on some individual dimension of quality (for example they are too expensive) or that the solution makes the wrong trade-offs across multiple dimensions (for example paying more for a product gets you higher performance, but you don't consider that extra cost worth it). In this case, the help wanted sign is the mismatch between how the customer defines quality and the solution's actual quality.

4. *Existing, high quality solutions*: this help wanted sign might, at first, seem illogical: If great solutions exist, why would a customer want something different? You need to consider that satisfaction with a current solution may be a kind of tunnel vision or *inability to imagine how things could be better*. Identifying this kind of help wanted sign can be harder than in the other cases because the customer often won't be able to tell you how things could be improved—but there are effective techniques for uncovering this kind of

information, and the effort to learn them is well worth it. (For more on this see www.marketdetective.com.)

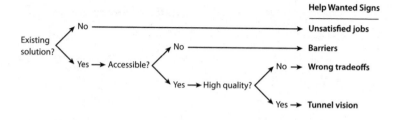

And that's it: the complete language you need to guide market investigations. To recap, the vocabulary of this language defines the information you're looking for. Once you've uncovered it and understood the interplay between the various elements (like how a specific customer's circumstance influences what *quality* means for solving a given job), you'll have the foundation for cracking a wide range of market mysteries.

Before moving on, it's worth commenting on how this applies when the customer you're trying to understand is not a person, but an organization or business-to-business (B2B) customer. These are by definition made up of *many* people, so you might assume that one-on-one conversations are not as relevant. In fact, talking to individuals within a B2B customer is essential for understanding the jobs the *organization* is trying to get done (you're not, after all, going to go talk to a building . . . at least I hope you're not . . .). However, there are a few distinguishing complexities to consider:

- When a B2B customer decides to hire a product or service to get a job done, there are often multiple people involved, what we call a *decision-making system*. As a consequence, you'll need to identify all the individuals who make up this decision-making system, understand the role of each in the decision-making process, and use this information to figure out who you want to speak with.
- For each of these individuals within the B2B organization, there are *two types of jobs* you want to understand:

  - *Role-based jobs*: these are jobs the person has *on behalf of the organization because of the role she plays in it*. For example, a CEO might have jobs like "create a high-performing leadership team," "develop a winning strategy," or "communicate strategy to the street." A person working in the HR department might have jobs such as "attract great people to work here" or "retain the great people we already have."
  - *Personal jobs*: these are jobs the person has related to personal goals and challenges. For example, this same CEO might have the personal jobs "leave a legacy," "convince the board I'm doing a great job," or "feel confident in the face of rapid industry change." The HR employee might have personal jobs such as "advance in my career," "develop my leadership skills," or "improve my work-life balance."

This means that for B2B customers, the work of the market detective involves the additional step of understanding the nature of the decision-making system, and the additional complexity of understanding both the role-based and personal jobs of the individuals in this system. However, once you understand these distinctions, it is straightforward to apply all the elements of our language.

To illustrate, let's imagine the customer of interest is the Tazza company, and we're trying to understand the aspirations and challenges of the organization itself. How does our language apply in this case?

Let's start by describing Tazza's circumstance and examine each of the four types of circumstance introduced above.

- *Situational*: For a B2B customer, time- and place-related variables are still relevant when defining the field of vision for your market investigation. For Tazza, we could specify the relevant time window as the few weeks leading up to the IPO. Or perhaps we'd expand it to the subsequent six months, depending on what we're interested in. The "place" would likely be the existing set of locations in the northeastern part of the country. The "while doing what" variable could certainly include relevant unfolding events, such as the IPO itself.
- *Demographic*: B2B customers have their own version of demographic descriptors analogous to those for B2C customers. For example, companies can be characterized by their life stage and financial status just like people can—and these factors are highly relevant to

the jobs they are trying to get done. Tazza is at the life stage of being at the inflection point of moving from a regional, high-growth company to a national chain. Other B2B life stages could be things like "start-up," "small business," "midsize company," or "Fortune 500 global corporation." Similarly, just like a person's financial status could be defined according to their savings, debt, readiness for retirement, monthly cash flow needs, and so on, these same factors are relevant to defining the financial status of a company. For Tazza, we might describe its financial status as "healthy cash flow but with tapering sales, and not enough capital to fund national expansion."

- *Identity*: Just as an individual might describe values, attitudes, beliefs, and affiliations that form parts of his identity, organizations have defining values, cultures, and affiliations. For Tazza, these might be values like "caring about customers as individuals" and "a sense of purpose related to creating and nurturing vibrant communities."

- *Agency*: Last, we might be interested in understanding the organization itself or some other group for which it has agency or responsibility. Examples of the latter could be its employees, the citizens of the community it lives in, its customers, or its shareholders.

OK, that covers the circumstance. What about the *jobs* Tazza is trying to get done? Here are some hypothetical examples:

- *Functional jobs*: often these are the most prominent type of job for a B2B customer. Role-based jobs could be "raise cash for expansion," "retain loyal customers," or "turn around declining sales," from CEO Cate Forrest's or CFO Elena Alvarez's perspective; personal jobs could be "advance in my career," from Head of Marketing Rob Butler's perspective, or "develop my skills and knowledge," from Jordan's perspective.

- *Emotional jobs*: for B2B customers, emotional jobs are always relative to individuals who are part of the organization. Consider the emotional jobs that Cate, Tazza's CEO, might have. She wants, for example, to feel confident that the company will be on a sound financial footing as it expands, and wants to reduce anxiety about the upcoming IPO.

- *Social jobs*: these can relate to how the organization wants to be perceived by its community (such as "be considered a responsible employer" or "show we care about the environment"), *or* can be at the personal level (such as "prove myself to my peers" or "demonstrate I'm a competent leader").

The other elements of our language, including what's currently hired, how quality is defined, and help wanted signs, apply in a similar way: as you understand the role-based and personal jobs of the various stakeholders, you can explore current solutions for their jobs, the criteria they use to evaluate and compare them, and where there are opportunities for improvement.

The Market Investigation Method

Now that you have a language to describe the information you're looking for about customers, the next thing you need is a method for gathering, organizing, and interpreting that information.

The backbone of the method I introduce here is a series of four, logically sequenced questions that you'll return to again and again. They organize the information you're seeking (as defined by the "Language" just described) and function as both a compass and roadmap for many market investigation techniques—above all, the one-on-one customer interview. To recap, these questions are:

1. What *circumstance* is the customer in?
2. What *jobs* is the customer trying to get done (in that circumstance)?
3. What is the customer *hiring today* to get those jobs done, and *why*?
4. What are the *help wanted signs*?

The logical flow of these four questions can be pictured simply.

Circumstances ——→ Jobs ——→ Current solutions ——→ Help wanted signs

As you answer these questions, you'll use the other elements of the language, like how the customer defines quality, the different types of circumstances (situational, demographic, identity, and agency) or jobs (functional, emotional, and social), and so on. To keep track of all this, it's helpful to organize the information you gather in what I call a job spec. It's worth committing to memory, as it forms a kind of mental roadmap for your customer interactions, whether these are one-on-one interviews or other types of interactions, such as focus groups, surveys, or observation.

Here's the completed job spec for Amelia, based on the answers provided earlier in this chapter (and in the story in Part 1).

Job Spec For: Amelia

Questions	Specs			
1. What **circumstance** are you in? • Situational • Demographic • Identity • Agency	**Zoom in:** • Late morning • After class • Weekdays • Alone	OR	• Saturday night • With friends	**Zoom out:** • Junior year of college • Pre-med • Single, female, extended family in another state • Has student loans
2. What **jobs** are you trying to get done? • Functional • Emotional • Social	• Get schoolwork done • Spend time with friends • Be entertained • Feel connected to family • Meet new people			
3. What do you **hire** to get those jobs done, and **why?** • Current solutions • Workarounds • Definition of "quality"	**Solutions** • Tazza • Library • Dorm • Bar/club/concert			**Definition of quality** • No distractions • Background "white noise" • Large space/big enough to be anonymous/hide in the crowd • Access to power for laptop • Not far from dorm/class
4. What are the **help wanted** signs? • Unsatisfied jobs • Barriers • Tradeoffs • Tunnel vision	• More access to power outlets • New people to meet • Better quality music			

Note that the four questions in the job spec are *not* the questions you're *literally* going to ask your customer. This may seem obvious, but it's so important that I'm emphasizing it here anyway. *These four questions are the guide for the information you are looking for; they are independent of the specific techniques you use for answering them.* That's why they are so helpful—and fundamental. In Jordan's words, "The questions you ask are not the questions you seek to answer."

OK, so how *do* you answer them? For the one-on-one customer conversation we're discussing here, there are three distinct steps:

1. *Imagine* what you will learn as a way to sharpen your focus going into the conversation.
2. *Investigate* with questions and prompts that inspire your interviewee to share things related to what you're seeking to understand.
3. *Interpret* what you learn by organizing and analyzing it in ways that reveal patterns and useful insights.

In practice, you'll usually cycle back and forth between steps two and three. You'll gather information, then interpret it, then use the resulting insights to guide additional investigation, followed by additional interpretation, and so on. This is why I've depicted these three steps using the visual of the detective's magnifying glass—as you cycle through the last two steps that form the lens, what you're looking for gradually comes into focus.

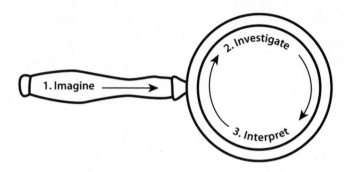

I'll discuss each of these three steps in a bit more detail.

Step One, Imagine, happens prior to your interaction with a customer or potential customer. The aim is to think in advance about the different categories of information you're looking for (helpfully organized in the job spec framework!) and imagine what you'll learn. In practice, this means filling out a job spec for your customer *before* you speak to her, with your *best guesses* as to what you'll learn.

At first glance this might seem like a strange thing to do; after all, isn't gathering the info to fill in the job spec the whole point of talking with someone? It is, but you'll find these conversations are more likely to be useful if you imagine in advance what you'll learn. For example, it will heighten your sensitivity to some of the clues dropped during the conversation—the ones that relate to your ingoing hypotheses (or guesses). Consider the perspective of Alex as he approached Amelia for the interaction with her. At that point in the story, he had the benefit of his conversation with Cate, during which he developed several hypotheses on the jobs Tazza was hired for, including creating a sense of community or belonging to the local environment. These would be natural hypotheses for him to test during the conversation with Amelia—who turned out to have very different jobs she was hiring Tazza to get done.

It will also force you to start thinking through, at this early stage of the process, the relationships between the different types of information in the job spec—and this can lead you to ask better questions. For example, if you know you're going to approach someone in a cafe to try to understand why he hires the cafe, you might hypothesize that situational circumstances, such as time, place, who he is with, or how far away he lives, are particularly important. You might also guess that his jobs to be done range from purely functional ones, such as "get an energy boost" or "eat breakfast," to social jobs, such as "spend time with friends" or "meet new people." These hypotheses could lead you to probe more on these types of circumstances and jobs to validate your ideas or understand them in more depth.

Of course you also need to be on guard against going into an interview with *too* much conviction that your guesses are correct. You need to remain open-minded about the possibility that they could be partly—or entirely—wrong. This is a careful balance you want to strike, and I'll come back to this in the section below on the right mindset to be in for these conversations.

Step Two, Investigate, is where most of the action happens, since you will venture into the world and talk to real people with the aim of gathering insights related to the problem at hand. Since I'm focused here on *how* to have these conversations, I'll assume you've already located a willing participant. (Much has been written elsewhere on how to design research programs and locate the right people to talk to; for a list of helpful resources, please visit www.market detective.com.)

A simple way to think about these interactions is as a series of prompts, provided by you, that inspire your conversation partner to share whatever they are comfortable sharing about the topics of interest. These topics, first and foremost, are the ones contained in the job spec, which therefore serves the dual purpose of roadmap and checklist. As the conversation unfolds, your role is to listen carefully and ask strategic follow-up questions to probe deeper or to clarify what you're learning.

You might assume that these interactions need to be precisely engineered or that there is a rigid formality to them. In practice that's not the case; great conversations have a tendency to meander in unexpected directions, and often those tangents prove to be the most interesting and valuable parts. This is why it's so important to distinguish between the questions you ask and the information you are looking for; as long as you have a clear view of the latter, you have a considerable amount of flexibility in how you obtain it.

Of course you *will* want to carry around an effective set of prompts in your market investigator's toolkit. I encourage you to experiment with many and to update them as you learn what works best for you. Here are some ideas to get you started:

- *Start with circumstances.* Look for insights into both the "zoom in" and the "zoom out" variables. Some things you may be able to observe directly, such as where a customer is, the time of day, what the customer is doing, or even basic demographic information. For others, you'll need to provide prompts to learn more. One extremely useful type of prompt is asking people to tell stories about different areas of their lives. These can be narrowly focused—for example asking them to narrate how they spend a typical day or even a slice of a day—or you can prompt them to tell broader types of stories, such as describing a typical week, month, or year, or a journey associated with some experience, such as buying a home or going through college. We saw several examples of this type of prompt in the story, for example when Cate told the story of how Tazza got its start. Stories like this are a rich source of insight and context, and help to build rapport and establish your interest early on in a conversation.

- *Ask why to uncover the real jobs.* As you listen to these stories, you'll discover lots of clues about a customer's motivations, problems, and goals. When these clues arise, the best follow-on prompt is the simple question "why?" Asking why—repeatedly, if necessary—helps you get to the deepest level of underlying motivation: the jobs the customer is trying to get done. Be sure to probe not just on the functional jobs, but on the emotional and social jobs as well. We saw an example when Alex repeatedly asked Cate why to uncover the deepest reasons underlying her decision to go to Italy: her search for a community and a place to call home.

- *Dig deep on current solutions.* One of the richest topics will be your exploration of current solutions and why they are not getting a customer's jobs done adequately today (or why they are). If there is a solution they are currently hiring, you can ask them why they chose it, what they like about it, what they dislike, and how it can be improved. It's also helpful to probe on what *else* they have hired for the same job, and again what they liked and disliked and what could be improved. Probing deeply on these topics—and forcing the interviewee to be very precise—will lead to a great many insights about how they define quality, how they measure it, and what trade-offs they are willing to make to get these jobs done.

- *Test for each type of help wanted sign.* While some clues about help wanted signs will likely be revealed in the course of probing on the first three job spec questions, it's useful to supplement those clues by systematically exploring each of the four types of help wanted signs: no existing solutions, barriers, suboptimal trade-offs, and tunnel vision. I often use these as a checklist to refer to toward the end of the interview to make sure I've covered all of them.

Step Three, Interpret, is when you analyze what you are learning. As you investigate, information will come at you fast, and you'll need ways to capture it, organize it, and understand its implications. Exactly how you do this depends, in part, on the nature of the problem at hand. But any tool for interpretation should reveal new insights, such as patterns or relationships in the data, and ideally spark ideas for how you might better solve for customer jobs.

Two such tools I introduced in the Tazza story are the job spec and the market map. I will focus on these here as they are both extremely useful and not covered elsewhere. (More commonly applied tools, such as customer profiles, personas, or customer journey maps, can also be quite helpful during the Interpret step. For a list of resources on these topics please visit www.marketdetective.com.)

The job spec and market map differ in their level of resolution. Job specs help you to understand what's going on with a single customer (or a single type of customer), whereas market maps help you to see patterns across multiple customers or customer types. A job spec, then, is usually more helpful for problems related to innovation or marketing, while a market map has broader applications in developing strategies and aligning organizations around a common purpose.

Using Job Specs for Interpretation

The job spec is more than a way to organize what you're learning as you explore the four primary questions of our method. One you've started filling it in, you can also use it to reveal new insights by asking interpretive questions such as:

- *Which jobs are highest priority?* In most conversations, you'll identify multiple jobs a customer wants to get done in a given circumstance. It's helpful to understand which of these jobs are the highest priorities (from that customer's perspective). All else being equal, a job is a higher priority if it's relatively *more important* to the customer, relatively *less satisfied* by current solutions, and would have a *higher value* attributed to it if it could be solved. Such jobs are often the best ones for innovators and strategists to focus on, because a lot of value can be both created and captured if they are solved.

- *Which jobs seem to bundle together?* It's common for customers to have more than one priority job they'd like to solve for simultaneously (again, in a given circumstance). This bundle often includes jobs from each of the three categories introduced earlier—functional, emotional, and social. We saw this in the case of Amelia, who wanted to solve for the functional job of getting her schoolwork done while also solving for the emotional job of feeling connected to her family. Understanding the full bundle is a great way to get more granular about what really matters, as it sets you up to design solutions or whole experiences that address the right mix of details.

- *How do different solutions stack up relative to how the customer defines quality?* If you've discovered multiple candidate solutions for the job (including those currently hired, those hired in the past, or those that might be hired in the future), it's valuable to understand in detail how each is evaluated. Getting a detailed view of how each candidate performs is a great source of insight into what quality really means in this context and the trade-offs the customer is willing to make.

- *What are the clear innovation opportunities?* Finally, it's helpful to keep track of any obvious opportunities for innovation that have arisen. Such ideas will inevitably surface either from the customers directly or as you consider the various help wanted signs that have appeared.

Using Market Maps for Interpretation

Market investigations are often motivated by the need to understand what's happening in the world on a scale broader than that of a single customer (or even a single type of customer). In these cases, talking to individuals is as valuable and essential as ever, but you'll need a way to make sense of what you're learning across many such conversations. This is the function of a market map. It allows you to visualize the broad landscape of where you play today, where your competitors are focused, and where there are threats and opportunities. They take some work to get right, but once you create a good one for your organization, you'll find it's a powerful strategic tool that has enduring value.

Any map starts with a set of primary coordinates. For geographic maps, these are usually latitude and longitude. For market maps, we use customer jobs for "latitude" and customer circumstances for "longitude." Locations on the map are therefore defined by the intersection of a circumstance and a job some customer is trying to get done within it.

As you talk to customers, you'll be able to fill in the jobs and circumstances you discover along the two axes of the market map. You can then mark the intersections on the map corresponding to the actual customers you've spoken with. It's helpful to code these intersections to reveal additional insights about the territory you're discovering, for example with a check mark to indicate the job is well satisfied today and an *X* to indicate it is not.

Here's the market map for Amelia from our story.

Market map for: *Tazza*	Circumstances				
	Amelia— Late morning	Amelia— Saturday night			
Get schoolwork done	✓				
Feel connected with family	✗				
Connect with friends		✗			
Be entertained		✗			
Meet new people		✗			

Jobs

In Amelia's case, there are two sets of circumstances in which she's hired Tazza, and five distinct jobs that are filled in on the axes. I've marked the job-circumstance intersections where a specific solution (in this case, Tazza) is hired. Check marks indicate it's a great solution for that job and circumstance, and Xs indicate that it's a mediocre or bad solution.

Completing this mapping and coding immediately yields interpretive insights into what's going on. For example, a Circumstance column with predominantly X marks likely means that circumstance is not a strategic one for the organization being analyzed, regardless of the job to be done. We see this on Amelia's map, as the Tazza cafe is not a good solution for any of her jobs in the circumstance of "Saturday night." Similar patterns often occur in the horizontal direction for specific jobs: lots of checks mean the solution is great across circumstances and therefore likely a strategic job for the organization to focus on; lots of Xs means it is likely not. For Tazza, an example of such a job would be the "eat a healthy meal" job, for which Tazza was not perceived as a strong solution in any circumstance.

The more complete your map, the more insightful patterns you can observe. Here are some of the most useful things to look for:

- *Who your real competition is.* Highlighting on the map where competitors get hired for the same job-circumstance intersections as *your* organization reveals your real competition. If your company is like most, this will likely be a much broader list than you originally think, and you might be fighting many very different competitive battles at the same time. In the story, this was a key challenge for Tazza, which was competing not only with other cafes, but with the fast-casual chain Santé for the job of eating on the go, and with the shared-workspace company Office Oasis for jobs related to getting professional work done or work meetings.

- *Why you get hired or fired today.* As we saw in the Tazza story, the patterns you can observe in market maps, combined with the detailed job spec insights from which they derive, reveal a great deal about why you win and lose today.

- *What your core market is.* Knowing which regions on the map are the best fit with your organization's offerings and strategy is an important insight that can often be derived from the patterns in your market map. Clearly any job-circumstance intersection for which your solutions are a good fit is a candidate for your core market, but also look for jobs you solve well across multiple circumstances, individual circumstances in which you solve many jobs, and areas where you have a clear advantage over the competition (or, even better, where there is no competition).

- *Where there are attractive growth opportunities.* Finally, there are likely many places on the map where you're not playing today (nor anyone else). These can all be systematically explored as potential opportunities for growth. Attractive areas are those where the jobs are highly important and highly unsatisfied as well as where there is a lot of value at stake if someone can solve them (either because *many* potential customers have the job, or relatively few do but they ascribe *a lot* of value to solving it).

As you apply the steps of this method, you'll likely go through several cycles of Step Two (Investigate) and Step Three (Interpret). Typically, you'll gather information, interpret it, realize more information is needed, investigate more, interpret again, and so on. But by following the interpretative strategies just outlined, gradually the solution to the market mystery at hand will come into clearer focus.

Getting in the Right Mindset for Understanding Customers

I've found four mindset principles that help make for a successful market investigation, ones I use personally during conversations with customers.

- *Be interested.* It may seem obvious, even strange to emphasize, but it's important that you be genuinely interested in the person you are talking with. In fact, this is the most important factor for a customer conversation going well; people love to talk about themselves, but only if they think the person they are talking to cares about what they have to say. Nurture your genuine curiosity about people, and unleash it when you are talking to customers.

- *Be authentic.* Your willingness to be yourself, and even to share your own situation and experiences where appropriate, is a great aid to establishing genuine rapport. It also helps you be empathetic, as you find and share connection points between what the customer is going through and your own life.

- *Have a beginner's mind.* Keep your mind open to whatever you might discover in a customer conversation, and allow these discoveries to guide where you explore further. It's often the hardest mindset for aspiring market detectives to implement, because it seems to conflict with my earlier guidance about the importance of imagining what you'll learn *before* you talk to a customer. In fact, you need a dual mindset that flips back and forth between simply taking in and absorbing information, in a nonjudgmental, sponge-like fashion, and then assessing what you've learned (so you can use it to guide your further questioning).

- *Just do it!* Rather than wait until you have the perfect market research design, perfectly formed hypotheses, or perfectly developed market detective muscles, just go start talking to customers! Of course, you want some semblance of a plan, but it doesn't need to be terribly sophisticated to get started. You'll learn so much by talking to people that you can rapidly refine your plan and home in on what matters most.

Parting Thoughts

Becoming proficient in the art of the market detective may seem like a daunting task, particularly if you are just getting started. There is a whole new language to remember, a new method and toolkit to master, and mindsets to adopt that come more naturally for some than others. And all while navigating the unpredictability of real, live encounters with customers!

Rest assured that anyone who invests the time and effort can be successful—and it is well worth it. I can attest to this from my own experience, as I progressed from rarely encountering customers in the wild to spending thousands of hours engaged in fascinating, inspiring, and often humbling conversations with them. This work has taken me around the world and allowed me to meet and learn from an extraordinarily diverse group of people. Over the years I have:

- Interviewed dozens of people living in small villages outside India's five largest urban hubs to understand the challenges they have taking care of their health—and the challenges of the country's healthcare system as seen through their eyes.
- Learned about the different perspectives of contractors, equipment rental companies, construction workers, city planners, and building companies as they all worked toward the goal of creating a new urban center inside one of the United States' largest cities.

- Traveled all across Italy speaking to nurses, cardiologists, and hospital administrators to understand their jobs to be done related to the purchase and use of heart arrhythmia devices for their patients.
- Spent several months in the midwestern United States studying the surprisingly broad set of functional, emotional, and social jobs people have related to feeding their pets.
- Visited some of the most high-tech sports stadiums in the world to understand how they created innovative, cutting-edge experiences to attract and delight their fans.
- Been moved by the stories of people who were gradually losing their hearing as they described their frustrations at not being able to communicate and live as they once had.

In all of these cases—and in many others—my goal was to understand the lives of customers deeply enough that others could use this knowledge to find ways to make their lives better. It is enormously gratifying when this is the result. If I can learn to do this, you can too. Success ultimately comes not from memorizing specific techniques, but from practicing a small set of principles—the principles I've described in this book. I wish you luck in mastering them, and in using them to crack whatever market mysteries you encounter in your career and life.

Acknowledgments

When I set out to write a book that teaches business ideas in the form of a fictional mystery story, I expected to encounter some skepticism (though in reality it emanated primarily from my own head). Thankfully, I received feedback from readers of my early drafts who encouraged me to continue. I owe a special thanks to my agent, Jim Levine, for believing in this project from an early stage and helping to find a wonderful home for it at PublicAffairs and Hachette. I'm also grateful for the early support of Mark Hussey, Mark Johnson, Jacques Goulet, Michael Ganz, Erika Meldrim, Alasdair Trotter, Elizabeth Entinghe, Prashant Srivastava, Jim Roth, and Carin Watson.

John Mahaney, editor extraordinaire, and the rest of the team at PublicAffairs have been fantastic collaborators. John's suggestions greatly improved the quality of this book and I appreciate his patient guidance through every step of the publishing process. Thanks to my friend Safi Bahcall for sharing his always brilliant advice on writing, publishing, and life.

Many others kindly took the time to read and provide feedback on my emerging manuscript, and for this I am very grateful. Thanks in particular to Scott Anthony, Craig Deao, Claudia Pardo, Bernard Kuemmerli, Katie Enos, Andy Parker, Shari Parvarandeh, Pontus Siren, Vinay Mehra, Roy Davis, Thiemo Werner, Josh Suskewicz, Aisaku Pradhan, Frank Capek, and Doug Shapiro.

I'd be remiss in not acknowledging the people and experiences who have influenced me as I developed my own ideas on the topic of "jobs to be done." Foremost among these was Clayton Christensen, who I was fortunate to have for many years as a colleague, teacher, friend, and coauthor. Clay was instrumental in popularizing the idea of jobs to be done and evangelizing its importance as a perspective from which to view the world. Clay sadly passed away as I was completing this book, but I've always kept in mind his example as a teacher, writer, and storyteller as the ideal to strive toward. I'm also grateful to the many clients and companies I've worked with and learned from over the years.

I owe the greatest debt of gratitude to my family. My parents and brother, Brian, have always supported me regardless of the divergent paths I've taken. I'd also like to thank my Rhode Island family, Ed, Claire, and Christine, for their love and support. Above all I'm deeply grateful to my wife, Suzanne, and my daughter, Zoe, who never fail to make me smile, inspire me, give me purpose, and remind me what matters most.

David Scott Duncan is a Managing Director at Innosight, where he works with leaders to help them create customer-centric teams, strategies, and organizations. He is a leading authority on the theory and application of "jobs to be done," with extensive experience conducting market investigations around the world.

David is the coauthor of two previous books, including the *Wall Street Journal* bestseller *Competing Against Luck: The Story of Innovation and Customer Choice*, written with the late Harvard Business School professor Clayton Christensen. Prior to joining Innosight, he worked as a consultant at McKinsey & Company and earned a PhD in physics from Harvard University. He lives with his family in East Greenwich, Rhode Island.

PublicAffairs is a publishing house founded in 1997. It is a tribute to the standards, values, and flair of three persons who have served as mentors to countless reporters, writers, editors, and book people of all kinds, including me.

I. F. STONE, proprietor of *I. F. Stone's Weekly*, combined a commitment to the First Amendment with entrepreneurial zeal and reporting skill and became one of the great independent journalists in American history. At the age of eighty, Izzy published *The Trial of Socrates*, which was a national bestseller. He wrote the book after he taught himself ancient Greek.

BENJAMIN C. BRADLEE was for nearly thirty years the charismatic editorial leader of *The Washington Post*. It was Ben who gave the *Post* the range and courage to pursue such historic issues as Watergate. He supported his reporters with a tenacity that made them fearless and it is no accident that so many became authors of influential, best-selling books.

ROBERT L. BERNSTEIN, the chief executive of Random House for more than a quarter century, guided one of the nation's premier publishing houses. Bob was personally responsible for many books of political dissent and argument that challenged tyranny around the globe. He is also the founder and longtime chair of Human Rights Watch, one of the most respected human rights organizations in the world.

.   .   .

For fifty years, the banner of Public Affairs Press was carried by its owner Morris B. Schnapper, who published Gandhi, Nasser, Toynbee, Truman, and about 1,500 other authors. In 1983, Schnapper was described by *The Washington Post* as "a redoubtable gadfly." His legacy will endure in the books to come.

Peter Osnos, *Founder*